Mothers at the Heart of Life

Sheree Phillips

Servant Publications
Ann Arbor, Michigan

Copyright © 1985 by Sheree Phillips

Cover photo © Erika Stone
Book design by John B. Leidy

Vine Books is an imprint of Servant Publications
designed to serve Evangelical Christians.

Published by Servant Publications, Box 8617, Ann Arbor,
Michigan 48107

All scripture references are from the New American Standard
Bible unless otherwise noted.

ISBN 0-89283-274-6
Printed in the United States of America

85 86 87 88 89   10 9 8 7 6 5 4 3 2 1

Contents

Foreword
 Larry and Doris Tomczak / xii
Introduction / 1

I. Laying Foundations
1. "I'm Having a Baby" / 5
2. Jesus First / 11
3. Husbands / 17
4. "What About Me"? / 23
5. It's OK to Need Help / 29

II. Caring
6. Love that Grows / 37
7. Children Are a Gift / 45
8. Homemaking: Joy or Duty / 51
9. Children Are Little People / 61
10. The Dangers of Comparisons / 69

III. Training
11. Children Take Time / 77
12. Do What I Say *and* What I Do / 87
13. Teaching: Assuming the Responsibility / 95
14. Loving Through Discipline / 109
15. The Fruit of Your Labor / 127

Further Reading / 139

This book is lovingly dedicated to my mother, Mrs. Elsie Pate. Your sacrificial love over the years has been and is the example I need to be motivated to lay down my life for my children. Thank you for always viewing motherhood as a special calling.

Acknowledgments

I WANT TO EXPRESS LOVING appreciation to friends whose labor of love made this book project possible: Pam Whitford, Karren McGlohn, and Linda Winner for the hours you spent typing and retyping each draft; Joe and Ann Grefenstette for your peaceful home which made such a warm atmosphere for writing; and Cyndy Grano for being God's special gift to me. Your sacrifice of time in editing and timely encouragement will never be forgotten.

And to Benny. How can I ever thank you for not only inspiring this project but also for constantly supporting and encouraging me. Without your patience, gentle (most of the time!) proddings when I got discouraged and unwavering faith in me, I would never have made it. Your example as a husband and father surpasses anyone on earth. I love you!

Foreword

"NOT ANOTHER BOOK on Christian family life!"

Many of us probably feel this way upon hearing of another "must" book on Christian family living. After all, haven't Christians written books about everything we need to know?

I don't think so. There is at least one area where there seems to be a void—but an increasing need as well. We have many books on motherhood written by older, mature women who reflect on their lifetime of experience and share their insights with us. These books are invaluable, especially for those who have little or no preparation for the challenge of parenting in today's society.

Now there comes a book for young mothers by a young mother whose insights and experiences are not drawn from yesteryear, but from yesterday. Her ideas are fresh as a batch of chocolate-chip cookies from your local mall (times have changed) and as enjoyable, too.

Today, there are approximately 78 million young Americans between the ages of 17 and 35. The future of our country greatly depends upon what happens to this "baby boom" generation. These young parents and parents-to-be need someone from within their ranks who understands their unique challenges and provides them with practical help. This is what Sheree Phillips does superbly in her book.

People of Destiny, a magazine we publish, featured an interview with Franky Schaeffer, son of the great theologian, Francis Schaeffer. We asked Franky, "What fields do you feel are the most pressing for Christians to begin to reclaim for Christ?" His response was immediate:

The most important field in the United States today to be reclaimed for Christ is the profession of homemaking. What America needs is hundreds of thousands of women who have the courage and faith to stay home even though it's unfashionable, women committed to work at raising their children in a godly home. Our only hope is the future generation, no one can train that future generation the way mothers can. So it is imperative that mothers, godly homemakers, become the heroines of the Christian movement and not be treated as if they are extra baggage.

If you are a young woman who identifies with these prophetic words or if you are simply looking for a practical handbook on the role of being an effective mother in our fast-changing culture, *Mothers at the Heart of Life* is for you.

We have known Benny and Sheree Phillips and their four children for many years. We can wholeheartedly endorse not only their book, but their lives. They have been an example to us of righteous living resulting in richer family life.

We commend the following pages to you. Our prayer is that you will discover the adventure of motherhood, amidst its many pressures and disappointments, to be a rewarding, high calling indeed.

LARRY AND DORIS TOMCZAK

Introduction

ONE COLD NOVEMBER NIGHT about eleven o'clock my husband, Benny, remembered he had left something in the car that he would need early the next morning. He bundled up and walked down the courtyard toward the parking area. Several single men who lived two houses down were having a party. As Benny passed their house, he noticed a young woman in her twenties on the patio with a child who looked to be about three years old. "I told you if I brought you here you better behave," she said, shaking him. "Either shape up or I'm putting you in the car. Understand?"

Another time the children and I were at a nearby grocery store doing some last minute shopping for a holiday weekend. With Jaime Sheree in the seat of the cart and Joshua in the back covered with groceries, we made our way up the last aisle toward the check-out lanes. Another mother with two small children came toward us, obviously upset with her older child who was cranky and irritable.

"Mommy, please let me get some gum," he pleaded.

In exasperation she said, "If you say one more word I'm gonna slap your face! Now come over here and shut up."

Sound familiar? These two heartbreaking illustrations vividly show the frustration that mothers today are experiencing over the responsibilities of raising children. How God's heart must break at such times as these.

We are facing an awesome challenge as Christian mothers of the 1980s. A well-known weekly news magazine did a feature on the American family that offered some shocking statistics concerning the state of our families. In 1980, only 13 percent of American families were considered "traditional": working father, mother at home, and one or more natural children. More than half of the mothers, totaling six million women, were in the work force. These mothers had a combined total of seven million children. One in every five parents was single, a rise of 40 percent since 1970. Abortions were happening on the average of every 30 seconds and two million children annually were victims of some degree of child abuse.

Recently much has been written about a new attack on the family of the eighties: abuse. A 1983 *Reader's Digest* article listed some startling cases: a seventeen-year-old dislocated his mother's shoulder; a fourteen-year-old vented her anger at her mother for not allowing her to go to a concert by stabbing her with a letter opener; a sixteen-year-old, confronted about poor grades, broke his mother's elbow.

The author, Cliff Yudell, reveals that thousands of children between ages three and eighteen "commit severe acts of physical aggression against their parents... deliberate, serious acts of violence that cause, or could cause, significant injury—incidents ranging from punching and kicking to hitting with objects or using a knife or gun... parents are actually living in fear of their own children."

What a tragedy! Yet thousands of years ago the prophet Micah predicted that this would happen. "For son will treat father contemptuously, daughter will rise up against mother, daughter-in-law against mother-in-law, and a man's enemies are the ones in his own household" (Mi 7:6).

It takes special grace to be a mother in this crucial hour. God desires that we rise above the darkness of the current attacks on the home in our country by opening our hearts to what his word has to say about our responsibilities, goals, and attitudes. The statistics are against us, but God is for us!

> All the days of the afflicted are bad,
> but a cheerful heart has a continual feast. (Prv 15:15)

> Trust in the Lord with all your heart,
>   and do not lean on your own understanding.
> In all your ways acknowledge Him and He
>   will make your paths straight. (Prv 3:5-6)

I remember riding in the car with my family years ago when my niece was a toddler. Dad had bought Deniece a box of Cracker Jack and she busied herself munching away and trying to assemble the toy surprise. Mom noticed her unsuccessful attempts to put it together and suggested that she read the instructions and tell Deniece how to complete her task.

"Grandma, I already read the directions," she explained.

"You did?" Mom chuckled. "What did they say?"

"They said you're just supposed to fool with it."

Over the years we have reflected on her answer many times. So often we neglect to take the time to carefully read the instructions to assemble a tricycle, bake a cake, or care for a plant. Therefore much time is wasted as we try our own way, only to end up with a lopsided tricycle, a dry cake, or a dead plant.

So it is with motherhood. So often we deem it unnecessary to "read the instructions," the word of God, thinking it couldn't possibly have much to say about raising children in the twentieth century. We then proceed aimlessly to try different methods to train them and ultimately end up just "fooling with it." Only the "it" in this case is a priceless human life.

Carole Mayhall uses an example that comically illustrates this point in the book, *Marriage Takes More than Love*:

> After an afternoon at the country fair, two country boys discovered they each had only a quarter left. One decided to ride the merry-go-round, but the other declined. When [he] finished..., he asked his friend why he hadn't ridden with him. The second boy replied, "Well, you spent all your

money, you got off where you got on, and you ain't been nowhere."

How frustrating it is to find ourselves on an emotional "merry-go-round" as we make attempt after attempt to become good mothers, only to eventually realize we "ain't been nowhere."

You and I are about to embark on a journey. We'll laugh and cry together, searching the scriptures to hear what is on God's heart concerning the awesome responsibility of being a mother. And I believe that we will both be changed when our journey is through.

Father, I thank you for the woman who is holding this book and ask you to anoint her heart and mind as we study the subject of motherhood. Give us teachable hearts and use your word to make permanent changes in our lives. Thank you so much. Amen.

ONE

"I'm Having a Baby!"

THE AMERICAN WOMAN HAS UNDERGONE vast changes in the recent decades. Many previously locked doors have been increasingly opened to us, especially in the area of career alternatives. Women are no longer limited to stereotypical jobs as secretaries, teachers, domestics, or librarians. Mothers who work outside the home are not labeled "negligent," because they are often motivated to seek outside employment just to help meet the basic needs of the family. More women are obtaining college degrees and moving into professions previously occupied exclusively by men. The obvious trend is toward women spending much money, often many thousands of dollars, and much time, sometimes years, preparing for a career that will ensure success, fulfillment, and financial security.

Why is it that we are encouraged to sacrifice time and money preparing for a career but are encouraged so little to prepare for motherhood? I am not lessening the importance of women being educated and trained to excel professionally. I thoroughly enjoyed college as well as my secretarial career. In comparison, however, it does seem odd that we are so eager to master the details of science and technology, and yet we assume that being a mother just "comes naturally." In some ways, this is true. Much of what a mother knows is instinctive, but this does not diminish the awesome responsibility of bringing a human life into the world and seeing that he or she becomes a functioning, mature person who will become a positive influence on the future of our society.

Preparing for motherhood is truly of vital importance, although not necessarily accomplished by attending expensive lectures or reading every book on child care ever printed. If you are anything like me, the preparation you need, or needed, was more in the area of attitudes, emotions, and spirit. Unfortunately, many of us had little of this type of training and were forced to learn some things the hard way. Nevertheless, God sees and understands our individual circumstances and prepares us in his way.

In her book, *Free to Stay at Home*, Marilee Horton addresses this important issue:

> I am not an authority on the sublime art of mothering, but am looking and learning from every source available. I wouldn't dream of showing up on a tennis court . . . and announcing, "I'm a tennis player." Not until I have learned how to play tennis and then practiced and practiced will I actually be a tennis player. In much the same way, mothering must be learned, developed, cultivated, and practiced. No one expects you to be perfect, but very few mothers who really give their best towards raising children fail.

All mothers have something in common. We all started out the same way. Whether it was an announcement we desired or dreaded, one memorable day we found out we were pregnant. I vividly remember the four times I learned I was pregnant with our four children: Joshua, Jaime, Jesse, and Joseph.

Benny and I married at age eighteen, and four and a half years later Dr. Crowe informed me that my most treasured childhood dream was becoming a reality. The joy I felt at that moment was almost more than I could take. I had just given two weeks' notice at my job, hoping that this could somehow be true. My heart was full of thanks to God and eagerness to share the news with Benny and our families. After all, five years is a while to wait for children, and they had been dropping hints for some time.

I reminisced about that night in June of 1977 when Benny and I prayed God would give us the gift of a child. Now, two months later, I was able to tell Benny our prayer had been answered. His response was all I had hoped it would be. We laughed and cried and thanked our God together. The closeness we felt to him and to each other was precious.

The next obvious person to tell was Mom. She was ecstatic! That evening I received a beautiful arrangement of pink baby carnations. Needless to say, her preference for a granddaughter was plainly declared.

My brother and Benny's parents and brothers were equally happy, but it was my older sister, Bonnie, who had the most moving response. When I told her the news, she cried tears that held more meaning than I was able to understand. You see, she was aware of something that I had never been told. Because of a potentially sterilizing childhood disease, my parents had been told not to expect me ever to have children. Bonnie had recently prayed that God would touch me with his healing power and give us a child. How I thank him for her prayer of faith and how I realized more deeply the wonderful miracle that was happening to Benny and me.

The following months were full of holidays and planning, decorating and shopping, but I thought April would never come. Each visit to the doctor I was sure he would say, "Anytime, Sheree!" but his response was always, "See you next week."

Finally, on April 12, 1978, at 3:30 a.m.—do babies ever come at sane hours?—I woke Benny up to call the doctor. It really was like the movies. "Hello, Dr. Crowe, this is Benny Phillips. My baby is having a wife!" Joshua Michael came six hours later, weighing in at nine pounds and five ounces. Benny and I shared the experience of watching our son being born and wept with joy. Some friends and several of our family were there to share our happiness in the recovery room, and my Mom didn't complain a bit that I was holding a blue bundle instead of pink.

The days and weeks that followed were both exhilarating and trying, but we made it. As each day passed, I was more aware of the dramatic changes a baby makes in a woman's life and marriage and I often cried out to God for his strength.

Then, just as we were beginning to feel secure in our new life as parents, God decided to bless us with a surprise. As Joshua turned just eight months old, we discovered another little "blessing" was on the way. My initial reaction was quite different than that of eighteen months before. I was thoroughly enjoying motherhood, but the anticipation of another child so quickly was overwhelming. My emotions were also clouded by morning sickness and fatigue. Bonnie smiled and said, "Boy, God really did heal you, didn't he?"

Fortunately, the physical adjustments came quickly, and in no time I was feeling the life within me. Joshua noticed my expanding body, and I had fun explaining that Jesus was giving us a new baby. I longingly admired dresses and lacy socks in the stores ("a girl would be nice, Lord") and began to dwell on the advantages of having children close together.

Jaime Sheree was born on September 27, 1979, at the more decent hour of 3:30 p.m. Once again we witnessed our loving Father bringing new life into our world, and my mom was delighted to shop for pink.

Potentially dangerous jaundice required that Jaime be rehospitalized several days after we brought her home. Seeing her in the incubator with a bandage over her eyes to protect them from the bright lights was almost more than I could take. Benny and I stayed with her but could hold her only during feedings. In just a few days she had captured our hearts and seeing her sick caused us much pain. Thank God, prayer works! In just twenty-four hours she was home, and the experience produced even more thankfulness to our God for this, another life.

I had no idea what the coming year would hold with two in diapers and days full of all the chores of homemaking and caring for two small children. "Lord," I would sometimes pout, "Why me? How am I to endure such a hectic life? Will I ever have time for just me again? Maybe working, at least part time, wouldn't be so bad after all. I didn't go to college to learn to change diapers. I thought being a mother was supposed to be like the magazine covers of pretty women holding their smiling babies! They looked happy enough."

How quickly I forgot the thanksgiving and allowed the circumstances to determine my attitude. Some days were so good and others so terribly bad. I suddenly realized how spiritually and emotionally unprepared I was to be responsible for other human lives. I finally turned to the scriptures, determined to overcome the inconsistencies and arrive at some level of peace and contentment. Surely the Father of all creation would help me to understand about being a parent!

I am thrilled to testify that he heard the cry of my heart and brought answers. Within just two years I even began experiencing the gentle stirrings of wanting another child, and in the summer of 1982 a desired but unexpected child was conceived. God's sense of humor is so delightful. In the middle of preparing a manuscript on motherhood I found myself pregnant!

On April 8, 1983, we again witnessed the miracle of birth when Jesse Merritt entered our world. We were further blessed with Joseph Charles on January 24, 1985. Each had excess amniotic fluid in his lungs, which caused respiratory distress and required an extended hospital stay. Both times we battled with anxiety, and resisting fear was a challenge. But both boys progressed well and soon I was home with four small children. With each new challenge comes the realization of the responsibility of fashioning a human life. With all of my inconsistencies and questions, I am comforted in knowing that my loving God is with me.

Lord, thank you so much that children are truly a gift from you. Remind me daily that you have entrusted them to me and that in my weakness you are made strong. Thank you that you never give me more than you and I can handle together and that your grace is always sufficient. I love you. Amen.

TWO

Jesus First

ONCE THERE WAS A MAN who decided to build a house. In his eagerness, he failed to be as concerned with laying a strong foundation as he was with completing his project as quickly and efficiently as possible. Finally, the exterior was finished. It was a beautiful colonial home, the house of his dreams. As the spring rains came and were followed by winter snows, the earth underneath began an invisible erosion of the weak foundation. Soon thousands of dollars were spent to save his sinking home.

In this same way, we busy mothers often desire immediate, visible results in our children, but we must realize that without a vital relationship with Jesus Christ we do not have the proper foundation. The emotional and physical strain of motherhood requires a strong spiritual foundation. It takes special wisdom and grace to raise children effectively in these tumultuous times.

The disciples once came to Jesus to ask what was the greatest commandment of the law. Jesus replied, "You shall love the Lord your God with all your heart, and with all your soul, and with all your mind" (Mt 22:37).

I was raised in a home where going to church was an essential part of my life. My earliest memories are of Sunday School, children's choirs and picnics with the pastor and his family. At a very young age I began to recognize my need to have a personal relationship with Jesus Christ. I knew that he was real, that he had died for my sins, and that the Bible was true. I said my prayers faithfully before meals and at bed and insisted on Mom reading my daily Bible story at night. In fact, Mom and Dad would often laugh at the memories of me standing in the pulpit on Sunday nights helping to "lead the singing" at age three.

As I progressed into my teenage years, I became more interested in being accepted and popular and less interested in the Lord. Although I continued attending church regularly, even when my family went through a period of not going, there was no zeal for the Lord in my life. My relationship with him was maintained more out of habit than loving desire. I was considered to be a moral young person, but few of my friends knew of the scriptural convictions behind my hesitance to go to their parties or indulge in some of their activities. In many cases, I did compromise my biblical convictions to ensure their acceptance.

My junior year in high school was a real turning point in my life. I suddenly began to realize that simply going to church wasn't filling the aching in my heart. Through a Bible study that began in our school, I experienced a dramatic confrontation with Jesus Christ that radically changed my life. His Spirit filled me with joy. I was eager to share his love with my friends, and Benny and I were able to lead many of them into a relationship with Jesus.

That teenage experience began a new life for me. Walking daily with Jesus became an adventure rather than merely a learned childhood behavior. Going to meetings was not a ritual, and my Bible didn't spend nearly as much time on the shelf between Sundays.

Have you made Jesus Christ Lord of your life? Can you reflect on that day when you surrendered control of your life to him, admitting your sinful nature and crying out to him for his forgiveness? Everyone must deal with these questions at some point in their lives. Without him it is impossible to function joyfully on a daily basis as a mother. If you have not yet received Jesus, my prayer is that you'll do so soon. You will never regret it.

Now that my responsibilities have increased to being a pastor's wife and mother of four, I am more aware than ever of my need to maintain Jesus as my first priority. Much has been written on the subject of walking in the Lordship of Jesus, but I have found that walking with him can be boiled down to one simple but important truth: our relationship with him, like in any other, grows only in proportion to the time we invest in it. Just as our friendships take a sacrifice of time and affection, so does our relationship with Jesus.

Jesus Christ often left the crowds to slip quietly away to be alone with the Father:

> And after he had sent the multitudes away, he went up to the mountain by himself to pray. (Mt 14:23)
>
> And when day came, he departed and went to a lonely place. (Lk 4:42)
>
> But he himself would often slip away to the wilderness and pray. (Lk 5:16)
>
> And in the early morning, while it was still dark, he arose and went out and departed to a lonely place, and was praying there. (Mk 1:35)

If Jesus, the Son of God, so fully realized his need to spend time alone with the Father, surely we must also recognize the awesome importance of regular time with him. It is in the intimacy of undistracted time worshiping and praising him that we sense his presence, hear his voice, and receive the strength we need to go on. Just as our bodies need nourishment through physical food, so our spirits need nourishment through time with the Lord and in his word.

Many of us know much about the Lord, but little of him.

During the time that I was dutifully attending meetings, singing in the choir, and serving in whatever ways I could, I was also void of any meaningful conversation with the Lord. In the privacy of my room my prayers were repetitive and dry, for I had little to say to someone I hardly knew. Only as I surrendered my whole being to him—mind, will, and emotions—did he begin to show me how to express my love to him. My inhibitions slowly decreased and I caught myself singing songs of praise to my God while driving or doing dishes. Oh, how we need to be released to express our love unashamedly to the Lord with all the worship he deserves!

As a child I heard the Bible described as "God's love letter to the church." As any young girl would, I could identify emotionally with this intriguing concept, but I had trouble applying it to the scriptures.

When Benny and I started dating in high school, he was not one for writing romantic love letters, primarily because we saw each other almost daily. The few times he did have occasion to write little notes or send cards I would read them over and over. The warmth and love I felt were wonderful. It was then that the Lord said, "Yes, Sheree, my word is my love letter to you, my daughter. If you will read it with this same enthusiasm and desire, I will reveal myself to you in an intimate way. I will cause your heart to grow toward me as a maiden's heart turns toward a man. And through my word I will refresh and teach you."

Being consistent to spend time with Jesus and devote myself to his word has been a recurring struggle for me, especially since becoming a mother. It's so easy to allow seemingly important things to distract my attention, but those times when I neglect to begin my day with Jesus are the days when I seem to run the fastest but accomplish the least. My temper is short, my time is less productive, the children seem to try my patience and, ultimately, the tears come. When I am faithful and consistent to cultivate my love relationship with Jesus by spending time in worship, prayer, and study of his "love letter" to me, I then have the resources I need to handle life's situations with the peace and wisdom that only comes from him.

> But seek first his kingdom and his righteousness; and all these things shall be added to you. (Mt 6:33)

Father, forgive me for allowing the responsibilities of life to distract me from you. I want you to be first in my life but I need your help. I desire to discipline myself in spending time with you daily and studying your word. Free me to worship you in the quietness of my private life and anoint me to understand the scripture. I want to get to know you, Jesus. Restore the joy of my salvation to me. I do want that love relationship with you. Amen.

THREE

Husbands

SEVERAL YEARS AGO I was visiting in the home of a woman from our fellowship and was impressed by a small plaque in her kitchen which said: "The greatest thing a mother can do for her children is to love their father." Reflecting on the truth behind this simple statement reminded me of my parents' relationship and how it affected me as a young child. Several pictures come immediately to mind: Dad bringing home an unexpected box of candy; Mom spending hours preparing a homemade German chocolate cake (and it wasn't even his birthday!); Mom and Dad walking hand in hand to the High's store to get an ice cream cone; Mom sitting for days at Dad's side during a frightening hospital stay. Yes, my parents had their share of struggles, but the love was always there. The security of knowing that Mom and Dad loved each other added more to my life than any other single factor.

As mothers, we must resist the unconscious tendency to allow our children to replace our husbands on our list of priorities. Many fathers have admitted feeling left out of their wives' affections because of the pressing needs of the children. Am I suggesting that we, therefore, neglect the basic needs of our children to attend to our husband's every whim? By no means. I am merely offering a reminder that God established marriage before he gave children. In Genesis 2:24 he said, "For this cause a man shall leave his father and mother and shall cleave to his wife, and they shall become one flesh." The full meaning of the Hebrew word "cleave" in this verse means "to glue oneself to." Many a marriage is deteriorating today because the parents have unintentionally allowed children to absorb so much of their time, affection, and energy that the glue between them is no longer sticky. As Dale Evans Rogers once put it, "They have forgotten to be sweethearts in the throes of rearing children."

First Samuel 1:3-9 offers startling insights into this principle. Elkanah was a godly man who loved his wife Hannah very much, but verse 5 says that the Lord had closed Hannah's womb. Elkanah's second wife was quite a woman. She had many children and did not cease to remind poor Hannah of this fact. Verse 6 says that she would "provoke her bitterly to irritate her, because the Lord had closed her womb." Hannah became so distraught over her state of childlessness that she refused food.

One day Elkanah, obviously distressed over his wife's anxiety, asked, "Hannah, why do you weep and why do you not eat and why is your heart sad? Am I not better to you than ten sons?" (verse 8). The Lord must have used this loving confrontation in Hannah's life because the next verse speaks of her rising to eat and drink. Although she experienced periods of hurt afterwards, God used Elkanah to reveal a truth to her about our foundation for maintaining proper priorities as busy mothers: God gave us our husbands before he gave us our children.

I was sharing on this verse with a group of women in a nearby city. After the meeting a woman asked that we pray for her.

"I don't have ten sons, but I do have five daughters," she said. "I want my husband to know that I love him and I realize that I've been neglecting him lately. Will you pray for me?"

As tears of joy and repentance came, we prayed and cried and thanked God for using his word to speak directly to her need. I left that day encouraged by her example. Seeing her desire to reestablish proper priorities gave me a new determination to do the same on a regular basis. The best thing we can do for our children is to love, respect, and continually cultivate our relationship with their dad.

What are some practical ways we can demonstrate this commitment?

1. *Express visible affection.* Visible expressions of love are vital for cultivating security in children. Our Joshua gets a real kick out of seeing Daddy give Mommy a sneak kiss or an affectionate hug at the kitchen sink. What a contrast to the type of upsetting behavior many children witness between their parents today!

2. *Set aside regular time alone together.* Several years ago Benny and I set aside Monday night as our "date night." We go out for dinner, see a good movie, go to a nearby park to swing, or just take a ride. We take this time to be alone together to communicate or just have fun. It has become a well-circulated fact that you don't call the Phillipses on Monday night. The children have already picked up on this. They know this is a regular part of our family schedule and look forward to spending time with my niece, who serves us by babysitting each week. As we, by God's grace, maintain this commitment and as the children mature, they will absorb the importance of our need to be together and appreciate that mom and dad actually *enjoy* one another. Jack Mayhall stresses the importance of married couples continuing to set aside regular time alone together:

> We have a price to pay for ... sharing in another's life. And the one payment that will yield the greatest interest is time together. Dates don't have to be costly, but the price must be paid in **Discipline** and in **Time**—the discipline of making it a priority, ... and of **Taking the Time**.

3. *Recognize him as the final authority in decision-making.* Recently people have been discussing at length the role of the

wife in the home. "Submission" has unfortunately become a misunderstood and abused concept. My intent is not to discuss this term in depth, for much has already been written for each of us to study and discern. I do believe in the concept of submission, for it is clearly biblical, but I do not support either the empty-headed, doormat extreme nor the militant, "Nobody tells me what to do" reaction. I appreciate what Beverly LaHaye, a noted seminar speaker and writer, says in *The Spirit-Controlled Woman*:

> Submission does not mean that [the wife] is owned and operated by her husband but that he is the head or manager. ... Christ's example teaches that true submission is neither reluctant or grudging, nor is it a result of imposed authority; it is rather an act of worship to God when it is a chosen, deliberate, voluntary response.

Ultimately, the husband is the final authority in the home as Christ is of the church. The wife is undoubtedly vital in offering her input and direction, but the children must see tangible evidence that their mother respects their father, even with his imperfections.

4. *Honor him in creative ways on special days.* My family always made a big fuss over festive times. Finances didn't allow for expensive gifts or extravagant parties, but when it came to making Dad feel special, we were pros. Birthdays, anniversaries, and especially Father's Day would often take weeks of planning. There were the gifts (often handmade), breakfast in bed, favorite goodies, lipstick greetings on the bathroom mirror, notes in the car, and anything else we could think of to let Daddy know he was the most important man in our lives. What memories this instilled in my young mind! Now I'm able to pass this enthusiasm on to our children. Children thrive on seeing that mom and dad love each other enough to go out of their way to show it.

5. *Pray for him as a family.* How I fail on this one! Although

prayer is a regular part of our children's lives, I neglect to stress with them the importance of praying for Benny. You might say, "But Sheree, your children are young. How can they really understand the concept of prayer anyway?" I believe they do understand to the limit of their capacity, and I also believe that a life of prayer will come only if a habit of prayer is learned at an early age.

Our husbands need our prayers! The tremendous temptations and responsibilities they face require a family who will stand behind them in intercession before the Father. Instead of being so quick to criticize their weaknesses, we would do better to first pray for them. Instilling this attitude in our children will produce more understanding and respect for their father in later years.

Lord Jesus, thank you for my husband. Give me the strength and wisdom to be the support and encouragement that he needs and cause our relationship to grow into one that will be a biblical example for those around us, especially our children. Give me creative ways to tangibly express my love for him, and help him to notice! Thank you, Jesus. Amen.

FOUR

What About Me?

DO YOU EVER FEEL like you've been locked into your home and someone lost the key? Whether it's emotionally, physically, spiritually, or all three, you feel that if you don't get some outside stimulation you'll turn into a jelly-brain. How about those days when the only stimulating conversation you have with an intelligent adult is when you discuss the newest methods of potty training with a neighbor?

After Joshua was born I was certain I had "arrived" at the place God created woman to be. Those initial days of nursing at 2 A.M. were sheer delight, perhaps because he started sleeping through the night at ten days. All the duties of diapers, baths, disinfecting his room, sterilizing everything in sight and proudly displaying him in the grocery store made me feel useful, fulfilled, proud, needed... and utterly exhausted. But even the fatigue was tolerable because my mother and sister were so helpful and supportive. Reading about the "postpartum blues" in women's magazines made me chuckle. "Sure I'm tired, but who could actually get depressed about having a baby? How silly!"

Then, with Joshua 16 months old and still in diapers and newborn Jaime just home from the hospital with colic, I reread those articles with a new appreciation. Some days I barely knew whether it was night or day, weekend or weekday. Then the guilt struck. "Lord, you've given me these beautiful children. Why am I so depressed? Don't I love them? What a terrible mother I'm turning out to be!"

Everything in me was crying out for a break. Jaime's incessant crying, my lack of rest, and having an active toddler were causing more emotional stress than pride allowed me to admit to anyone. I suddenly remembered my sister mentioning that she had faced similar problems after her second child, Douglas, was born. "Surely, Bonnie will come and rescue me," I thought.

When I called, Bonnie was very understanding. "I know exactly how you feel, Sheree," she responded. She explained in more detail the struggles she had after Douglas came and assured me that she made it through with no permanent scars. What encouragement! She also agreed that I could use a short break.

"Terrific!" I thought. "Now she'll offer to come and help with Jaime for a few days."

"Tell you what I'll do," she said. "I'll come by after work and take Joshua home with me for the weekend. How's that sound?"

"Bonnie, I can deal with Joshua. It's handling Jaime that's the problem. What's wrong with me? If you could just take her and give me some time to . . ."

"Sheree," she interrupted. "I'll be by to get Joshua at 5:30. I love you. Bye!"

I don't think I've ever been so upset with my sister! How could she be so insensitive? What good would it do to take Joshua anyway? I would still have the crying, the two-a-night feedings, and the fatigue. At least Joshua would be away from his cranky mother and have a few days with Bonnie and Mom. When she came by that evening, I was still hurt and confused. It wasn't until weeks later that I understood what my sister had done.

You see, the times we tend to run from our responsibilities are the very times we need to press in and face them. Elisabeth Elliot says, "Evasion of responsibility is the mark of immaturity." If Bonnie had relieved me from dealing with my expanding family, I would have probably begun an unhealthy emotional pattern of withdrawing when things got too difficult. By forcing me to face my circumstances, she helped me to avoid the additional guilt of seeing others cheerfully handle *my* God-given responsibility. That weekend alone with my new daughter began a relationship that has become priceless to me. The lesson also prepared me for the same kind of adjustments after Jesse came.

James 1:2-3 says, "Count it all joy, my brethren, when you encounter various trials, knowing that the testing of your faith produces endurance." When we endure the trials of motherhood, we allow the Holy Spirit to produce patience in us. Yes, running from them can produce temporary relief, but this inevitably leads to immaturity, guilt, and low self-esteem.

The postpartum blues do pass with time and loving support from family and friends, but the commitment to raising those babies doesn't pass, and it does become more time-consuming. That's when many women, frustrated with the daily boredom of motherhood, resort to returning to an outside job, throwing themselves into soap operas, or simply becoming an emotional frazzle.

Take time to look back: whatever happened to those old friendships, hobbies, community volunteer activities, and spontaneous shopping sprees (even if it was just looking in the windows)? Remember how good it felt to take the time to spend a leisurely lunch with a friend? The initial adjustment and time commitment of motherhood forces us to drop those things which formerly occupied our time. Certainly we may need to discard some of those interests permanently, but we must resume those relationships and activities which are important and God-ordained to avoid the emptiness of feeling left out and detached from others.

We must not feel guilty for having needs ourselves! Yes, the Lord and our family are our highest priorities and we cannot neglect them to hop from Bible study to volunteer work to exercise classes, selfishly excusing ourselves under the guise of

"I have needs too!" On the other hand, how many well-meaning women have found themselves lonely, middle-aged, and living with a husband they hardly know anymore because they devoted themselves exclusively to motherhood? Once the children are in college or married, those women suddenly find they have no life of their own, and they become bitter and resentful because the children don't write or call often enough.

How can we maintain personal interests without neglecting our God-given priorities? Only you and Jesus can properly reach that balance in your life, but let's discuss some areas in which you can prayerfully begin getting involved.

1. *Develop friendships.* Why are adult friendships so difficult? A recent survey suggests that only one in ten adults have a "best friend." As young people in school we were more available, had more in common, and had more choices for friends than as mothers at home. In addition, young people are typically more honest and transparent, so that adult friendships tend to be more superficial through years of pride and busy schedules. Friendship is dear to the heart of God. He understands our need for companionship. One of the reasons he created mankind was for this very reason. Do you have that special friend to turn to for support, encouragement, and companionship?

> A friend loves at all times and a brother is born for adversity. (Prv 17:17)
>
> A man of many friends comes to ruin but there is a friend who sticks closer than a brother. (Prv 18:24)

Pick up the phone and call that special person you haven't made time for. Tell her you love her and miss her friendship and set up a time to get together this week. You'll feel better and she'll be so pleased!

2. *Develop hobbies.* Most women have a natural creative instinct, so we often enjoy various kinds of hobbies. Whether it's tennis, crocheting, reading, playing the piano, painting, or

refinishing furniture, we find relaxation and personal fulfillment in doing something we enjoy. As mothers, we need the stimulation of resuming these activities and even trying new ones. Time is precious, I know, but even if we set aside a few hours a week while the children are napping or in school, we will feel refreshed by doing so. Often we can use this time to make our home more attractive or to make gifts for a new baby or a relative's birthday. Be adventurous! Try something new and experience the delight of personal accomplishment. You will suddenly realize that your hands know how to do something besides change diapers and scrub bathtubs.

3. *Spend time alone.* I adore my children and I love to be with them, but will you be too surprised to know I look forward to nap time? Sometimes I like to curl up in bed with the phone disconnected after taking the older children to mom's (to their delight), and putting the baby down for a nap. I can then bask in quiet! Mothers need time alone to read, to walk, to listen to a favorite album, or just to sit and enjoy the silence. This is when an understanding husband, neighbor, family member, or friend is indispensible. If naps are few or not a good time, someone must be with the children while we take a little break. Don't feel guilty! In this case, a break is not an attempt to run from our responsibilities, but rather a healthy need to spend time exploring ourselves and our personal interests. When we've completed our responsibilities, maintained our priorities and scheduled our time wisely, we can turn to others with a clear conscience and say, "I'd like a break. Can you help me out?" Try it. You'll like it, and your family will be blessed to have mom back refreshed, relaxed, and ready to tackle a new week.

Lord, could I have been feeling down these last months simply because I've been neglecting myself? You know how hectic my life is one day and how boring it seems the next. Help me to pursue friendships, hobbies, and time for myself without neglecting my precious family. I trust you, Jesus. Amen.

FIVE

It's Okay to Need Help

THE FIRST TIME I TAUGHT on the subject of motherhood, a young mother of an active toddler approached me and said, "Sheree, I appreciate your insights, but I've felt guilty turning to someone else for help. It was even hard for me to come here today because I didn't want people to think I was a bad mother who needed to be rescued. Thanks for letting me know it's okay to need help."

This woman was facing a very common predicament. We so often feel that turning to others means we are admitting failure and weakness. This feeling is true especially in the area of motherhood, because it reflects on the very core of our capabilities as a woman. Many mothers today are fighting hopelessness because they feel alone in their efforts to raise their children. Often the father is uninterested, uninvolved, or working long hours, and the mother's loneliness and frustration are taken out on the innocent child. Child abuse, neglect, and alienated affections can be the sad result.

In earlier times when a woman had a baby, her mother was usually the first one there cleaning, cooking, and seeing to the needs of the older children. Often neighbors or friends would supply meals or offer to serve in practical ways. My grandmother had eight children, five of whom were daughters. Those five daughters gave her a total of twenty grandchildren, and with few exceptions she was there helping after the birth of each.

Our society has unfortunately evolved away from this type of shared involvement. Chances are that you live far from close relatives, and are uninvolved in the lives of your neighbors. A neighbor of ours recently had her baby hospitalized and we didn't know it until she was back home. We interact even with Christian friends only at meetings. Isolation like this does not allow the deep relationships that we so need and desire. No wonder we often feel alone, wondering if we're the only women experiencing such struggles.

This is where the body of Christ, the church, comes in. There is a growing vision on the part of concerned believers across the world to restore the patterns established by the New Testament church. Several passages in the Book of Acts give us an exciting glimpse of their shared lives.

> And they were continually devoting themselves to the apostles' teaching and to fellowship, to the breaking of bread and to prayer. And everyone kept feeling a sense of awe; and many wonders and signs were taking place through the apostles. And all those who had believed were together, and had all things in common; and they began selling their property and possessions, and were sharing them with all, as anyone might have need. And day by day continuing with one mind in the temple, and breaking bread from house to house, they were taking their meals together with gladness and sincerity of heart, praising God, and having favor with all the people. And the Lord was adding to their number day by day those who were being saved. (Acts 2:42-47)

> And the congregation of those who believed were of one heart and soul; and not one of them claimed that anything

belonging to him was his own; but all things were common property to them. And with great power the apostles were giving witness to the resurrection of the Lord Jesus, and abundant grace was upon them all. For there was not a needy person among them, for all who were owners of land or houses would sell them and bring the proceeds of the sales, and lay them at the apostles' feet; and they would be distributed to each, as any had need. (Acts 4:32-35)

Somewhere along the line the church lost this kind of radical commitment to the Lord and to one another. The early Christians had a clear sense of responsibility to each other. When Julian, a pagan Roman emperor, faced the visible reality of the life of the New Testament church, he said, "[These people] feed our poor in addition to their own." Doubtless, this type of sacrificial love to others began within the Christian community. As they shared their resources, their time and their love, the world was forced to admit the startling reality of the God they served. Do we not serve the same God? Can we, then, do less than to seek to emulate the depth of relationships that our New Testament brothers and sisters shared?

Many of us come from traditional backgrounds where going to church meant attending meetings and pleasantly smiling while nodding a greeting to those in the pew in front or behind us. Someone recently called this "fellowshipping with the back of someone's head." At 11:50 everyone began checking their watches and promptly at noon the closing hymn was complete. The pastor moved to the rear of the sanctuary to shake hands with his parishioners, some of whom had just been awakened by the elbows of embarrassed wives. People came and went, often with broken marriages, teenagers on drugs, or hearts filled with loneliness and fear, but always projecting the attitude, "I'm doing fine and how about you?"

We as mothers raising children in the most crucial time in history often react the same way. Whether it's pride, fear of rejection, or countless other hindrances, something prevents us from admitting we need help. As we more fully realize our responsibility as the church to "have the same care one for another" (1 Cor 12:25), the love we share and the unconditional acceptance we cultivate will melt away these fears. We will laugh and cry together, knowing that our inadequacies will not affect our commitment to and love for each other. What freedom! If you are involved in this kind of Christian fellowship, consider yourself blessed.

1. *Overcome an independent spirit.* Many of us are simply too independent to admit we need input from others. This is actually an indication of insecurity. The "I don't need anybody" facade is merely a different way of saying, "I need you so much I'm afraid to let you know" or "Yes, I need input and advice but I can't bear to admit my failures."

Several years ago a small group of young women from our fellowship met for an informal Bible study in our home. The topic I shared on was "Why Women Need Other Women." After the teaching we were discussing how mothers, specifically, need the support of other mothers. A close friend of mine began to cry, humbly admitting that recently she had been fighting feelings of frustration and anger with her two toddlers. Discipline was becoming harder, and she was full of guilt and despair. Several of us were able to comfort her by saying, "It's okay, I know exactly how you feel." Being able to admit her weakness led to the comfort of knowing she wasn't alone in her struggles. In her book, *Open Heart, Open Home*, Karen Burton Mains warns us against "working hard to keep people from recognizing our weak points [because] we also prevent them from loving us in our weaknesses."

"[She] who conceals [her] transgression will not prosper, but [she] who confesses and forsakes them will find compassion" (Prv 28:13).

2. *Pray for a humble and teachable heart.* There is something refreshing about a person with this kind of attitude. In our community one of the first qualities the pastors look for in potential leadership is a heart willing to receive correction and

adjustment, for there you will also find a person willing to admit his total dependence on the grace of our Lord Jesus.

> A man's pride will bring him low, but a humble spirit will obtain honor. (Prv 29:23)
>
> Pride goes before destruction, and a haughty spirit before stumbling. (Prv 16:18)
>
> Where there is no guidance the people fall, but in abundance of counselors there is wisdom. (Prv 11:14)
>
> Where pride comes, then comes dishonor but with the humble is wisdom. (Prv 11:2)

The older my children get, the more I realize how much I need the input of others to help me learn to care for them. Mothers with husbands have the advantage of having an adult in the home to both encourage and lovingly admonish them. This type of help need not be limited to your husband. There are several mothers in my life whom I have invited to "speak the truth" in love to me (Eph 4:25). I desire both their encouragement and their correction. I know that they care about me and my children and have asked them to point out any improper attitudes or behavior in my life that would negatively affect my children in any way. I'm still learning to receive their observations joyfully, knowing that resistance is usually a sure sign that they are right. Just knowing they are available and concerned helps relieve some of the pressure of responsibility. Without the support and honest appraisal of your family and friends, the pressure could be too much to bear.

Single mothers desperately need to know that others are available to share with them in this way. Our congregation is divided into home fellowships that meet regularly. We encourage the couples in leadership who have single mothers in their groups to take special interest in caring for them. We also encourage those mothers to seek input and advice aggressively from their leaders and from others they respect. The church must not neglect to offer this kind of biblical ministry to the growing number of single parents in our society.

Having a humble, teachable heart is vital in the life of a mother who desires to be all God wants her to be. None of us has the ultimate answers concerning how to effectively raise children. Each of us can offer unique insights into various aspects of motherhood and together we will come to the well-rounded wisdom that only comes in an abundance of counsel. Gone are the days of "I can do it alone." May we each begin to pray for hearts that will humbly admit our weaknesses and cry out to God and others for help. Our children's lives are at stake. One day when I was in prayer I sensed the Lord putting it to me like this: "Sheree, until you learn to crave admonition as much as you do encouragement, you'll never become the woman I desire you to be."

3. *Do not be intimidated by wiser, more experienced mothers.* Low self-esteem is one of the greatest problems among American women today. The media and our desperate search for personal identity have drawn us into making unhealthy comparisons with others. If we are honest, sometimes we may want to look like the beautiful, seductive women wearing designer clothes on television or to act as self-sufficient as many in the feminist movement. Mothers are certainly not exempt from this. We look to others on Sunday morning and unconsciously envy their seemingly perfect children, always obedient, clean, and polite. We observe a mother who appears so creative, patient, and collected. Our ultimate question becomes, "Lord, what's wrong with me? Why are my children so rowdy and unresponsive with traces of peanut butter always smeared on their cheeks? Why am I impatient and out of sorts all the time?"

Titus 2:3-5 gives a powerful challenge to women in the church. Among the responsibilities of the older women (older in this case refers not only to age but to experience), verse 4 instructs us to "encourage the young women to . . . love their children." The Lord knew we would need training in the area of motherhood; we need not be humiliated by having to ask for it. Why not approach that mother you so admire and ask her and the children for lunch one day soon? I think you will make several discoveries. First, you'll see her children with peanut butter on their faces. Second, you may find that she struggles with many of the same inner frustrations that you do. Third, maybe the Lord will lead you into a relationship where you can humbly glean wisdom and insight from her life to strengthen and encourage yours. You may also find you'll have things to offer her in return.

Loving Father, forgive me for my independent spirit. I admit that I need the input of other more experienced mothers. Give me the grace to overcome any pride in my life and give me a teachable heart. Lead me to women that I can learn from and use me to affect positively the lives of others. I need this so much. Amen.

SIX

Love That Grows

IN THE LAST SECTION I discussed how laying proper foundations is the beginning of creating an environment that will produce contented, well-adjusted, and responsive children. Now we can begin to explore the practicalities of caring for them. This begins with love.

Including a chapter on "love" in a book on motherhood may seem somewhat strange to you. After all, what mother doesn't already love her children? Our society has so polluted the definition of love that we must be willing to reexamine this misunderstood concept. As we consider what the scriptures teach us about love, I hope that you will realize that we could all use some growth in this important area.

The Bible says that love is not a choice but rather a commandment:

> Beloved, let us love one another, for love is from God; and everyone who loves is born of God and knows God. The one who does not love does not know God, for God is love.... And this commandment we have from him, that the one who loves God should love his brother also. (1 Jn 4:7-8, 21)

Even before our children were born, Benny and I would confess our love for them. When he would leave for school or an appointment, I would get a kiss and my tummy would get an affectionate tap. "I love you both," he would often say.

The first time we saw our children it was unquestionably "love at first sight," wrinkled skin and all. Those first days were so wonderful, with meals in bed, nurses to call on, and a baby who constantly slept from the exhaustion of labor and delivery.

Then reality struck. The first night we brought Joshua home I was beside myself. Suddenly he was awake and announcing his arrival to the entire neighborhood. I tried feeding him, changing him, singing to him, and rocking him. The more I tried the more he cried. Fortunately, my Mom had come to stay with us for a few days. After a while she offered to take him so I could try and get some sleep. When I woke up a few hours later, I found her and Joshua on the couch downstairs, sound asleep. That experience taught me two important lessons. First, a new mother needs a lot of rest to deal calmly and patiently with a baby. Second, a mother's love must be unconditional or the trying times will ultimately cause us to resent our children unintentionally.

Our society has drastically reduced the meaning of love. To many, love is something that is determined by a racing heart, goosebumps, and "fireworks." It's an emotion that comes and goes. When it's there, you respond and when it leaves, you find someone else to conjure up the feelings. This we call romance.

A parent's love is not based on feelings or emotions. It is not affected by the response of the child. It is the closest earthly similarity to the love God showed us when he sent his only Son to die for us.

Unfortunately, many mothers today are not giving this kind of unconditional commitment to their children. Improper examples, selfishness, and fear of rejection are a few possible reasons for this. Our "me first" mentality often makes us so self-centered that we are unable to look past our personal interests and ambitions and to lay down our lives for our children. When they meet up to our expectations, we are selfishly motivated to "love" them, but when they disappoint or embarrass us, we feel less than godly acceptance of them. When friends or family are around we are on our best behavior: patient, understanding, and hoping they notice what good mothers we are. In the privacy of our homes, however, we often allow very different attitudes to surface. This is not unconditional love. In her book, *I Am a Woman by God's Design*, Beverly LaHaye addresses this issue as it especially pertains to mothers when she says:

> The term *mother* in the Hebrew relates "to the bond of the family"—the one who binds the family together. How necessary it is for a mother to learn to love her children, so the family might reap the results of her love.

The New Testament Greek speaks of three basic kinds of love. *Eros* is passionate, sometimes lustful love. *Philia* is brotherly love that says, "I like being with you." *Agape* is God's self-sacrificial, unconditional love. Guess which word is used in the passage from 1 John, chapter 4? *Agape.*

First Corinthians 13, often referred to as the "love chapter" uses this same word. A woman once shared with me a remarkable lesson that God taught her through this passage. He taught her that proper attitudes toward her children are essential.

Judy is the mother of two grown daughters. When her daughters were teenagers, she eagerly consented to try anything to ensure their happiness. She felt that to "love" them meant to do whatever was necessary to fulfill all their desires. She worked hard learning to sew to make fashionable clothes and often dropped everything when they needed a new outfit for a special occasion. Keeping them happy at all costs became her goal.

Then she heard what 1 Corinthians 13 says about love: "Love is very patient and kind, never jealous or envious, never boastful or proud, never haughty or selfish or rude. Love does not hold grudges and will hardly even notice when others do wrong" (verses 4-5, Living Bible).

Suddenly Judy realized that her outward attempts did little to actually show love for her daughters as described in the Bible. Giving the girls all of the "things" she could provide was worthless compared to treating them with patience, kindness, unselfishness, politeness, respect, and forgiveness, areas that she had not thought about improving. When faced with God's definition of love, she was forced to admit that some changes were necessary.

Stop and read this passage over once again, inserting your name each time you see the word "love." It's a good test. Like Judy, you will probably realize that love is not something we can assume we have in its fullness for our children. It's something that takes commitment and time to mature. How I thank God for those he has put in my life to learn from. They are "training" me truly to love my children (Ti 2:4).

As we allow the Holy Spirit to convict us of our lack of sacrificial, unconditional love, we can then begin more effectively to demonstrate this change to our children. Below are a few of the many ways we can practically do this, knowing that they need outward proof of our love on a daily basis.

1. *Verbal Assurance.* "Better is an open rebuke than love that is concealed" (Prv 27:5). Children need regular verbal assurance of our love. This has become quite a challenge in our house, as we are constantly thinking of new ways to say how much we love each other.

Our Joshua has always been very verbal for his age, and even at two he could articulate himself in very creative ways. His favorite phrase was "I love you too much!" and he would always dramatically hold out the word "too" for longer and longer periods.

"Honey, you mean *so* much, don't you?" I asked one day. "No, Mommy. I love you so much my heart hurts. That's too much!" he responded, while I laughed through tears.

As our children get older, there can be a tendency to minimize the importance of saying that we love them. I remember how often my dad would call me at home or work just to say, "I love you, Princess." What warmth and security that brought.

2. *Physical Touch.* Research has proven that humans need physical affection to develop normally. Babies who are fed by propping a bottle up in the crib and touched only when necessary become emotionally anemic. This need for touching extends past infancy even into adulthood. There is nothing more reassuring than an affectionate hug or a gentle caress, especially when it comes for no special reason.

Jesus understood the emotional security that comes from touching. In Mark 1:40-42 we read the account of his healing a leper. In Bible times, lepers were social outcasts. Leprosy was believed to be so contagious that it was feared by all, so lepers were often confined to isolated areas. When this man approached Jesus for healing, verse 41 says that Jesus was "moved with compassion" and "he stretched out his hand and touched him." We can safely assume that this diseased man had not been touched in a long time. Jesus' compassion was likely motivated not only by his illness, but also his need to be reassured by a loving touch.

Touching our children lets them feel our love. A squeeze on the arm, a pat on the head, or a hug does wonders for their self-esteem.

3. *Encouragement.* I have often heard this word defined as "to put courage into." In a day when being a moral young person is so difficult, our children need regular doses of courage. I once read that becoming a responsible parent means learning to be an encouraging parent." What a challenge it is to provide our children regularly with the encouragement they need!

Joshua has a strong but quiet temperament. He has never enjoyed being in crowds or getting a lot of attention from strangers. Since he was a baby, he has had a curious interest in drums. So, for his third Christmas we decided to get him a miniature but complete drumset. From the beginning he was a natural. He would carefully listen to Christian albums, waiting for the right moment to hit the cymbal and concentrating on keeping the beat. We clapped enthusiastically when he crashed the cymbal at the end of each song and told him how wonderful he had done, hoping that our neighbors shared our excitement with his newfound interest.

Because of his sometimes shy personality, we were surprised when he began to ask to play for friends that came by. Their enthusiasm produced obvious pleasure on his face. We realized that it was the encouragement he was receiving that built his self-confidence, which culminated when he asked to help "lead worship" at our Sunday morning gathering. He handled it like a pro and the congregation was thrilled. His next goal was to play at "Saturday Night Alive," a weekly teaching and worship ministry that Benny and I were involved in, where the average attendance was over 700 people. Our son is a living testimony of what encouragement can do.

> Finally, brethren, whatever is true, whatever is honorable, whatever is right, whatever is pure, whatever is lovely, whatever is of good repute, if there is any excellence, and if anything worthy of praise, let your mind dwell on these things. (Phil 4:8)

4. *Comfort*. Comforting our children is another way to assure them of our love. Isaiah 66:12 speaks of God comforting us the way a mother comforts her child.

Many times this maternal responsibility comes naturally, as when a child falls and scrapes a knee or when a teenager experiences rejection from a friend, but at other times our initial reaction is not that of comfort.

I love plants. Unfortunately, I have quite a reputation for letting them die of malnutrition or neglect, but I honestly do enjoy them. Jaime likes them too, but during the toddler years she was more curious about the dirt than the plant, so not touching them was a rule in our house.

When she was about two years old, I was in the kitchen when I heard her cry out in pain. I dropped the dish rag and ran to find her on the floor stroking her foot, with dirt from my favorite plant deposited all over the carpet. I wanted to say, "I told you not to play in the plants, now look what happened!" But the word "comfort" quickly came to mind. I was reminded by that voice inside to comfort her, pray for her foot where the plant had fallen on it, and only then reprimand her for her disobedience. Comforting our children lets them know that they are more important to us than things.

5. *Laughter.* So many times we get distracted by the discouraging condition of our society that we neglect to realize the importance of laughter in the family.

It has often been said that the husband sets the *pace* in the home and the wife sets the *mood.* I have found this to be true in our family. My mood, whether good or bad, ultimately affects Benny and the children. Laughter really can be the best "medicine" for a difficult situation. We must be sensitive, however, about when to laugh and when not to laugh. We have two station wagons, a large nine-passenger one and a smaller compact version. Jaime recently wanted to know when the smaller one would "grow up" to get big like the other one. We all laughed heartily and she was obviously thrilled. We explained that cars don't "grow up" like children and praised her for her creative little mind. Our laughter in this case was fun for our daughter. But laughing at your children's first attempts to draw a house or to ride a bike, however innocent your motives, can be emotionally devastating to them.

Children love to laugh and ours are no exception. Hearing them giggle with delight while they attack their daddy on the living room floor does wonders for our family life. Who can keep a straight face while hearing someone laugh from deep inside? My brother, Jon Mark, used to have a contraption called a "laughing box." You pushed a button and a battery-operated voice would laugh hysterically. We had so much fun taking it places, putting it under dad's pillow or just turning it on in the middle of dinner. Inevitably, everyone ended up practically in tears as we laughed not only at this silly toy but also at each other.

Laughter shows our love by assuring our children that we actually enjoy them. Knowing that they can bring joy to mom and dad builds their feeling of self-worth. This is where God's *philia*—love comes in, that brotherly affection that knows how to relax and enjoy the other person. We must not let our responsibilities as mothers prevent us from being fun to be with even if it means three rounds of "Candy Land." Let's ask ourselves this question: "Am I the kind of mom I would like to have had?" Having fun with our children will help tremendously.

> Better to live in the desert than with a quarrelsome, complaining woman. (Prv 21:19, Living Bible)
>
> When a [woman] is gloomy, everything seems to go wrong; when [she] is cheerful, everything seems right.
> (Prv 15:15, Living Bible)

In later chapters, we will be discussing other important aspects of loving our children (including discipline, providing for their physical needs, and respecting them), but verbal assurance, physical touch, encouragement, and comfort are some ways you can begin today to express your love for them.

> *Jesus, it's so good to know that love takes time and that I can grow in love for my children. I want to love them with your sacrificial, unconditional love, always having their best interests at heart. Forgive me for being impatient, unforgiving, and unkind, and help me to begin to express my love to them in creative ways. I want so much to grow and I admit I need your help. Amen.*

SEVEN

"Children Are a Gift"

IF YOU COULD SURVEY a group of a hundred mothers asking them, "What made you decide to have children?" you would probably get a hundred different responses. Let's allow our imagination to speculate on some of those:

"My husband and I desired to have a visible expression of our love to one another."

"All married couples have children, don't they?"

"God told mankind to be fruitful and multiply."

"I always wanted to be a mother. It's like having a living doll to play with and care for."

"I didn't decide to have a baby and I wish it had never happened."

"Mom wanted grandchildren and Aunt Bessie was beginning to think something was wrong with me after six years and no kids."

We could go on for hours wondering why couples choose to have children, but suffice it to say that each of us has our own reasons. Unfortunately, none of the above statements offer a guiding principle for bringing a new life into the world. Consequently, when our expectations of having immaculate, perfectly behaved, responsible children are exploded by reality, we have no real foundation to insure against unrealistic expectations and disillusionment. We often blame our children for our inability to raise them effectively.

In order to help avoid some of these negative patterns or correct an already existing one, let's examine two foundational truths from the scriptures concerning children.

Children Are a Gift from God

The Psalmist wrote, "Behold, children are a gift from the Lord, the fruit of the womb is a reward" (Ps 127:3).

The word *gift* in this verse could be literally interpreted as an "assignment" or "heritage." They are our personal assignment from the very one who created them, and he will personally hold us accountable for how well we do this task. During those precious moments of seeing them take their first step, perform their first recital, or snuggle up for a good night hug, this is easy for us to accept. Other times we have to consciously force ourselves to admit they are a gift.

One evening Joshua and Jaime were playing happily downstairs while Benny and I were upstairs hurriedly dressing for a fellowship gathering. We suddenly realized that the normal noises that accompany our two energetic toddlers had stopped. From previous experience we knew this meant trouble. Whenever they get too quiet we know that mischief is inevitable. As Benny quickly moved down the hallway to the stairs he detected a strange but familiar smell. "Baby powder!" he shouted. The children knew they had been discovered, so they quickly dropped the evidence, but they had already "cleaned" the living room tables, "waxed" the floors, and "washed" Jaime's hair. Benny found them in a cloud of powder dust, and Jaime's eyelids had the only remaining trace of flesh color on her face. For weeks afterward we wiped dust off furniture, daily washed Jaime's hair, and explained the peculiar odor in our home to our friends.

At moments like these it's good to be reminded that children truly are a gift from our loving Father. Already, we are learning that the most difficult moments tend to become our most treasured memories. We must resist the temptation to view our children as a nuisance, an interruption, or an inevitable by-product of marriage. They are our very special gifts, hand-picked for us straight from the throne of God. He has chosen them for us and us for them. The miracle of conception alone should startle us into the joy of knowing how wonderfully dear they are.

Let us agree with Eve in Genesis 4:1 when she said, "I have gotten a . . . child with the help of the Lord."

God Exhorts Us to Rejoice over Our Children

"Let your father and mother be glad and let her rejoice who gave birth to you" (Prv 23:25).

"He makes the barren woman abide in the house as a joyful mother of children. Praise the Lord!" (Ps 113:9).

Mothers today experience the elation of the birth of a child differently than women in the recent decades. In my mother's day, motherhood was an expected occurrence, usually as soon after marriage as possible, whereas my contemporaries are choosing to have fewer children or none at all and are waiting longer to start their families. Mom made all her doctor visits alone and went through labor in a room full of women, most of whom had elected to be completely knocked out to avoid the pain. She was whirled to a delivery room full of strangers. After the delivery a masked nurse informed Dad of the new child in a father's waiting room on another floor while the baby was whisked away to the nursery. World War II prevented him from even seeing my older sister until she was over a year old.

I, on the other hand, was encouraged to bring Benny to office visits so he, too, could hear our unborn baby's heartbeat. We went to six weeks of parent preparation classes at the hospital, and he coached me through labor with few if any pain-relieving drugs. We watched our children's births and were able to hold them in the recovery room for family and friends to come and see.

Mom was thought of as strange for choosing to nurse her

babies; breast-feeding is now becoming the more accepted way to nourish newborns. She was hospitalized for up to ten days, seeing us only at daytime feedings, while my babies were with me almost constantly during my three-day stay.

While many mothers are experiencing the birth of a child as an exciting, chosen event rather than an expected one, other women are obviously deciding not to have children or are terminating their pregnancies by abortion. Since the 1973 Supreme Court decision, seven times more babies have been aborted in this country than men were killed in the Revolutionary and Civil Wars, World Wars I and II, and the Korean and Vietnam Wars combined.

Somehow we as Christian mothers must come to a place of realizing the pricelessness of each human life, especially those that God entrusts to us personally. We must not resent them for interrupting our careers, cramping our style, distracting us from personal interests, monopolizing our time, or interrupting our lifestyle. A popular woman's magazine recently featured an article in which several different new mothers were interviewed regarding the adjustment of juggling a career and being a mother. One of the women and her husband had just bought "an old house in need of a lot of loving personal care" when their child "intruded" on their lives. Notice the house needed the loving care and the child was the intrusion.

These selfish attitudes will ultimately be absorbed by our children. The emotional scars they could receive would cause immeasurable damage. Raymond and Dorothy Moore, respected authorities on the issue of the family, agree with many leading psychologists that "the child who feels rejected is usually more damaged than the one who is physically bruised."

In our day-to-day lives as mothers, we have to understand that being joyful is different from being happy. Happiness is an emotion. Joy is an inward state of being, proof that the spirit of God dwells within us (Gal 5:22). Therefore, happiness is an *outward* manifestation and joy an *inward* reality. We should not feel guilty when we aren't happy when Bobby comes in covered with mud from head to foot or a teenager admits to getting a bad grade on a test. We must obviously handle such situations with the correction and reproof we deem necessary. However, the inner quality of joy at God's gift of that child should not be shaken by the often frustrating trials.

The attitudes we have toward our children are by personal choice. One instance when I experienced this challenge occurred when Jesse was three months old.

I had been sick for several days and had been unable to sleep. Emotionally and physically I was exhausted. On Sunday morning Benny encouraged me to stay home to rest while he took Joshua and Jaime to our meeting. I eagerly agreed and was looking forward to two hours of blissful sleep while Jesse napped.

Well—guess what? He decided to skip his morning nap to energetically exercise his lungs. Nothing I did satisfied him, and soon I joined him in tears, tense and frustrated. Resentment soon followed—toward Jesse for interrupting my needed (and deserved, I thought) sleep and even toward Benny for not having to deal with the responsibility of two toddlers and a newborn on a daily basis. Needless to say, I was not happy at that time.

Suddenly I realized I was failing in my "assignment" miserably. I had a choice to make. I could either continue in self-pity or rise above the circumstances by faith. The decision was a hard one. I wanted to rest and, yes, I wanted to feel sorry for myself. But that quiet voice inside me reminded me that Jesse was a precious gift from God not meant to be a burden but a blessing. The choice was mine.

How I needed the grace of God at that moment! Soon his strength became evident in my weakness. I got up, cuddled my son and affirmed my love for him in a new way. After a long time of pacing, rocking, and singing he fell asleep just as Benny and the children got home. After lunch all of us had a wonderful nap.

The attitudes we have toward our children are by personal choice. We can choose to view children as an interruption or as an inconvenience. Or we can choose to be challenged by God's exhortation to receive our children as precious gifts given specifically to us by the God of the universe and to rejoice over them individually. My prayer is that we will adopt the latter view. If so, the responsibility of joyfully receiving them doesn't end when the doctor announces their arrival in the delivery room, it only begins there. We must remind ourselves a dozen times each day that they are each priceless to the Lord and to us, not only when they behave properly, but also when they unnerve us. For, in like manner, we undoubtedly disappoint our heavenly Father, and yet he so lovingly and joyfully accepts us, his children!

> *Father, thank you for my children. Forgive me for forgetting how blessed I am to have them, and remind me daily to thank you for them. I confess that they are a gift from you and commit myself to rejoicing over them. Teach me how to develop a joyful spirit so that my home will be one filled with happiness. In Jesus' name. Amen.*

EIGHT

Homemaking: Joy or Duty?

THIS SECTION ON CARING for our children deals with many important subjects: our need to love and respect them, to recognize that they are delightful gifts from a loving God worth rejoicing over, and to refrain from consciously comparing them to others. In this chapter we will be considering an obvious but vital area of caring for our children as we examine our responsibility to provide for their physical needs. Because of the abundance of material available that gives practical ideas in this area, our emphasis will be on having proper attitudes rather than outlining the "ten steps to creative homemaking."

Performing the daily functions of operating a home can lose its appeal soon after a woman is married. As the weeks turn into years, the joy of cleaning, cooking, and doing laundry for a new husband or baby is lost as a feeling of duty sets in. If left unchecked, this attitude can soon develop into a sense of worthlessness for the homemaker, and she often seeks contentment in other areas. Homemaking responsibilities are then considered to be chores: the sooner they're done the better. Many women turn to a dependency on convenience foods and other short cuts which deprive the family of necessary nutrition and care that are essential to health and happiness in the home. Then when a neighbor has a death in the family or a friend has a baby, we eagerly prepare a meal for them or set aside time to clean their house with unexplained enthusiasm. Karen Burton Mains asks:

> Why is it always easier to extend the courtesies of hospitality to those outside our immediate families? Husbands, housemates, children . . . often receive short shrift of our kindly attention.

I sometimes reflect on our foremothers and the picture I get is one of a strong woman wearing a long dress, her hair in a bun on the back of her head, sweat lacing her forehead. She's been over a steaming pot while a fine mist of dust is settling in the room where she has just swept the dirt floor. Clothes are hanging on the line outside and the iron is on the fire heating to starch white shirts, calico dresses, and sheets. I wonder, "How did they do it?" as I load the dishwasher and rush downstairs to get the clothes out of the dryer before they wrinkle.

As contemporary women, we have many distractions that can interrupt our daily lives: the telephone, the television, the latest novel or fashion magazine, a nearby shopping mall, unexpected guests, and others. It is so easy to put scrubbing the bathroom floor off until tomorrow when a friend calls and wants to meet you for lunch or Sears is having a sale on children's pajamas. These interruptions are not always bad. I often have an important phone call or a friend stops by in need of prayer or a shoulder to cry on. But more often, I find that I allow unnecessary things to conveniently distract me from household responsibilities. ("But honey, I just *had* to finish that book before the children accidently flushed it in the toilet.")

Joyfully attending to the physical needs of our families does not mean that we are to forsake everything to attend to their every need. Rather, we are to order our priorities so that our God-given mandate as mothers to care for their needs in the home is met, even when the Lord has other plans for us. Proverbs 31 is one I read when I sense a need in my life for conviction in the area of homemaking. Verses 10 through 31 address the responsibility of a wife and mother to see that her family is properly clothed, fed, and cared for. It also speaks of the attitudes a *godly* woman exhibits and the response she will receive from her grateful husband and children. Verses 17 and 27 offer an important insight concerning this important ministry: "She girds herself with strength.... She looks well to the ways of her household, and does not eat the bread of idleness."

When I consider the word "idle," I immediately think of "lazy." In the hectic life of a wife and mother, there is little time for laziness, right? It depends on your definition. If laziness means sitting in front of the television watching a soap opera, a Coke in your hand and the house in a mess, then no, the conscientious homemaker has no time for such. But if your definition is one of neglecting God-given responsibilities to pursue selfish whims, whatever they are, then yes, I must admit to being lazy at times.

Lack of vision in the home has caused me to be discontent and restless and has forced me to battle feelings of uselessness. What do I mean by "lack of vision?"

When an artist is asked to paint a portrait, he naturally must first spend many sessions with the subject. He observes, sketches, observes some more, sketches some more, and so on. Many sittings later a detailed likeness in oil appears on a formerly blank canvas in a beautiful blend of colors and shadows. Whether his subject was a person or a mountain landscape, the result depends on what he has spent the most time observing and striving to duplicate as vividly as possible.

So it is in the life of a mother. Each of us has at some time had a picture in our hearts of the kind of woman we hoped to be. From childhood most of us dreamed of the family we would someday have. We imagined what marriage and motherhood would be like and even had ideas of what our husband, children, and home would look like.

Unfortunately, if you are like me, you focused so much on the outward things that you somehow neglected to set goals for what you desired to be on the *inside*. When marriage and motherhood do not meet our expectations, we are left with the disappointing feelings of disillusionment, apathy, and hopelessness.

The Bible gives us a picture of the type of character qualities and attitudes we should be cultivating to become the godly women he has called us to be. The type of sacrificial love and unconditional acceptance Jesus Christ has for us, *his* children, is the best model we have. Picture it. We are the subject, God is the artist. If we allow God's hand to guide the strokes on the page, the image that is produced as he observes and sketches us reveals the likeness of Jesus!

As we allow his Spirit to convict and change us, we will be able to forsake our selfish concepts of motherhood (especially homemaking) and absorb a fresh vision of the kind of outlook we should have. We can change! The more we cooperate with God, the more he is able to help us overcome unbiblical habits and attitudes. Imagine that! You can be a different person in a short time if every time you are tempted to resent your homemaking responsibilities you choose, rather, to thank God for the opportunity to serve your family with a willing heart. Day after day, in chore after chore, this new attitude will slowly produce a natural new perspective.

In this way, we can begin to get a new "vision" of our responsibilities and as we seek to attain it, it becomes more accessible. As our vision of ourselves becomes one of fulfilled, energetic, and creative homemaker without unrealistic expectations, contentment is the delightful result. Whatever we allow our vision to be will determine what will appear on the canvas for all the world around us to see. By observing and desiring to duplicate what the scriptures say about having a happy home, as well as by seeking to learn from the example of godly mothers in our lives, we will each be better equipped to make the vision God places in our hearts a reality.

If you are a Christian woman, then Paul's exhortation to "work hard with gladness . . . as though working for Christ, doing the will of God with all your heart" (Eph 6:6, Living Bible) is an excellent verse to begin to apply in the area of homemaking. God has already placed a picture in your mind of what he can do in your life. He will honor your desire to submit to his will in this area and equip you to fulfill those seemingly mundane tasks with renewed energy.

After the Lord restored my vision as a homemaker, disorganization was the next area I tackled.

Benny and I are complete opposites in many ways: he's a blond and I'm a brunette, he tends to avoid conflict at all costs and I can be argumentative, he's more structured and I'm more spontaneous, he loves schedules and I detest them. For years he tried to help me resolve the frustration of running from morning to night and still feeling unproductive by encouraging me to organize my time into a schedule. "Spontaneous me" resisted, claiming that schedules made me feel stifled. Uptight and exhausted, I continued to fall into bed at night fighting guilt because I never did get to the ironing.

After years of resisting his simple solution, I weakened and developed a schedule. I kept it somewhat flexible and didn't post it on the kitchen wall, but it was a schedule. Each morning of the week I had time for exercise and time with the Lord. The afternoons were blocked out for meetings with sisters, outings with the children, writing or regular maintenance cleaning. Late afternoons were set aside for cooking and evening for free time, hospitality, or meetings. A typical week in my weekly planner may look like this:

	Sunday	Monday	Tuesday	Wednesday	Thursday	Friday	Saturday
Morn	Corporate Meeting	Family Day	Laundry/ Bedrooms	Jaime at Ballet/ Shpg	Kitchen/ vacuum	Leaders wives mtg.	Baths
Afternoon	Rest		Home Schooling	Home Schooling	Home Schooling	Home Schooling	Home Schooling
Eve	Lutyks for Dinner	Evening w/Benny	Time w/ Pam	Home Mtg.	Leader's Mtg.	Free	Hospitality

Taking into account the inevitable interruptions and temporary set-backs due to a child's not feeling well or an unexpected emergency, I soon began to feel much more productive as an organized routine became a part of my hectic life. This became especially important when we decided to educate the children at home. The schedule didn't smother me as I had expected, it freed me to say no to unnecessary distractions, and actually gave me more time to pursue personal interests. Soon I was even carrying a pocket calendar which is always full, but nevertheless, saves me from the embarrassment of "Oh, I'm *so* sorry, I forgot!" Time management is still a recurring struggle for me, but having a schedule has helped tremendously. It has also been a real blessing to Benny!

Being open to help from others has been equally important to my productivity in our home. My mother is always willing to help out with the children or the housework when her schedule permits. (During my third pregnancy she came over weekly to do the heavy cleaning.) Friends in our fellowship have also been available to serve our family by babysitting, helping with preparations for a special dinner, or showing up unexpectedly to mow the yard. Allowing others the joy of giving isn't always easy, but it certainly makes a difference to have some help, especially during the hectic times.

Schedules are not just important for mothers, they are equally as important for children. Routine helps them to feel secure, insures that they are getting adequate rest, develops discipline and order in their lives, and brings peace to the home.

I am amazed at the number of mothers who struggle with overly active children and think nothing of allowing them to stay up at night until they literally fall to sleep on the living room floor. Certainly some children need more rest than others, but it is important to the children (and the mother) to be on a schedule that requires at least a rest period during the day and regular mealtimes. Again, flexibility is important when circumstances require it, but too often we are quick to interrupt our children's lives to pursue a selfish interest and then end up frustrated with *them* because they are cranky and irritable. How many times have you gone out somewhere and thought, "I should have just stayed home!" Even if you are the mother of older children, you must not minimize the importance of maintaining order and peace in the home by beginning now to provide them with the structure they so desire.

When naps, meals, or outings are slightly delayed we should certainly be flexible and not feel like we have neglected our children, but every effort should be made to maintain their schedule even when we have to rearrange ours. A very helpful practice for us has been to train our children to be able to sleep at others' homes. This makes it possible to take them with us almost anywhere we go without having to adjust their sleeping schedules. Although it was tedious at first, we were able to persist, and now they will sleep almost anywhere. What freedom it is to be able to visit a friend over a leisurely lunch or share with a couple over a late dinner while the children are sleeping!

First Corinthians 14:33 tells us that our God "is not a God of confusion but of peace." Order in the home will bring the peace we so desire and we will refrain from disciplining our children's unruly behavior when we are possibly to blame for not providing them the schedule they need.

Many women fight feelings of depression and frustration when it comes to homemaking. The responsibilities of cooking, cleaning, laundry, ironing, shopping, and the many other factors of keeping an efficient home can be overwhelming. Recently I came across a startling insight into a frequent reason for these feelings in my life.

In Genesis 4, we read the account of Cain and Abel making their sacrifices to God. God was pleased with Abel's offering but not with Cain's (v. 5). Cain's response was that he "became very angry and his countenance fell." In other words, he was depressed.

Verse 7 reveals an amazing truth in God's response to Cain, he said, "If you do well, will not your countenance be lifted up?" The implication here is that when we do well, we feel well.

A woman's self-concept revolves to a great extent around her home and family. When our home is orderly, we feel good. I love the smell of disinfected bathrooms and polished furniture, yet sometimes I don't get to them on schedule. When the reason is justified, I simply get to it when I can. If I have been irresponsible, I feel convicted. I react defensively to Benny, battle with discouragement and feel basically lousy. Even if it means canceling personal plans, I always feel better when the house is tidy and the laundry is done. Built into every person is the satisfaction that comes when we take our responsibilities seriously.

With renewed vision, a fresh commitment to organizing our lives more effectively, and some free time to pursue personal interest, we will be better prepared to tackle the responsibilities of homemaking with a willing attitude. God promises that "his grace is sufficient . . . for power is perfected in weakness" (2 Cor 12:9). The times we feel the most inadequate are the times his strength is most available.

Jesus, sometimes I do feel overwhelmed and frustrated by the daily routine of being a homemaker. Thank you for showing me that part of the reason may be because I can sometimes be irresponsible.

Forgive me for the times I have neglected these God-given responsibilities and thank you for refreshing my vision. I commit myself to becoming more organized and I trust you to give me strength to serve my family with joy. Amen.

NINE

Children Are Little People

MY OLDER BROTHER, RANDY, was quite a character. Because of his wonderful sense of humor and outgoing personality, he was loved by many people. When I was fifteen and he was twenty-one, he broke his neck in a tragic swimming accident and for the remaining five and a half years of his life he was a quadriplegic. I learned so much from him during those years, enough to fill another book, about having compassion and respect for those whom society often neglects. But the people he taught me most to respect were children. Randy always called them "little people." He didn't use this title to insinuate that the word "children" is demeaning or disrespectful. It was simply his way of lovingly reminding himself and others that people are people, no matter how small. He knew all too well how it felt to be viewed as less than worthy of respect, because his wheelchair existence forced others to look down to communicate with him.

"Kneel down, Sheree," he would often say when I was talking to my niece or nephew. "It's no fun for them to have to look up all the time."

It wasn't until after he went to be with the Lord that I realized the reality of that statement in his life. It's thrilling to know that he no longer has to constantly look up to others. There are no wheelchairs in heaven!

Our adult-centered culture has made some very demeaning references to children. They are typified as being "snotty-nosed rug rats" who are "better seen and not heard." They have sometimes been the object of jokes and comic strips depicting them as "menaces to society."

The word of God, however, gives quite a different picture of children. We have already learned that they are each precious gifts from God who are worthy of our rejoicing. The greatest tribute to "little people" was given by Jesus.

The disciples were often concerned about who among them was the most important to Jesus. Although they loved him, they also loved themselves and were eager to know how their relationship to Jesus would affect their future position in heaven. The mother of James and John even got in on the act and asked Jesus to give her sons a very special place of honor (Mt 20:21). Jesus' answer wasn't quite what any of them expected, but then, his will for our lives is often not what we would choose for ourselves. In Matthew 18:3-7, he gave an amazing answer when asked who would be the greatest in the kingdom of heaven.

He said, "Truly, I say to you, unless you are converted and become like children, you shall not enter the kingdom of heaven. Whoever then humbles himself as this child, he is greatest in the kingdom of heaven. And whoever receives one such child in my name receives me; but whoever causes one of these little ones who believes in me to stumble, it is better for him that a heavy millstone be hung around his neck, and that he be drowned in the depths of the sea."

Jesus clearly understood the value of children on the earth and he insisted that we become like them to experience his saving grace. Causing just one of them to stumble is worthy of punishment in the heart of our God.

Psalm 139 offers a beautiful look at God's omniscient care for us, even before we were born:

For thou didst form my inward parts; thou didst weave me in my mother's womb. My frame was not hidden from thee, when I was made in secret . . . thine eyes have seen my unformed substance. (vv. 13, 15-16)

Oh, the love of God for little people! Every human life is precious to our Creator. My brother had clearly absorbed one of God's foundational attitudes toward children: he respects them. Webster defines respect as "high admiration or esteem for a person or quality, polite regard or consideration, courtesy, and deference."

How important is respect to a child? Let's find out by considering some positive qualities that come from being respected.

1. *Healthy Self-Image.* Each of us struggle with accepting ourselves. Children are no exception. Even at an early age they learn that to be accepted they must run the fastest, wear the most fashionable clothes, and own the newest stereo equipment. Our goal as mothers should be to assure them that they are precious to us and to God, not because of what they have or how well they perform, but because of who they are.

Often, this means that *we* must first grasp this important truth before we can effectively instill it in our children. Do you often struggle with feeling worthless and nonproductive. If so, join the ranks of a majority of American women who have been highlighted in many women's magazines by admitting to feelings of low self-worth. Dr. James Dobson, respected authority on issues of the family, has said that low self-esteem is the greatest cause for depression among women. Feeling like we must strive to be noticed and accepted by others by using various attention-getting devices, such as wearing sensual clothes, starving to lose excessive amounts of weight, or using various means always to be the center of attention models an unhealthy example for our children. What we are silently communicating is, "Honey, if you expect to be loved and appreciated in life, you must do all you can to get attention.

Living up to others' expectations makes you worth something."

Pause briefly and consider how contrary this worldly attitude is to the nature of God. He counted you to be worth the life of his own Son. Even before you were born he knew your name, and he loves you just the way you are—inconsistencies and all. Yes, he hurts when you reject his will and disobey his commands, but he promised he would always lovingly correct you and never leave you. He also actually commands you to love your neighbor "as yourself."

Now, as you meditate on this life-changing principle, he can in turn give you the strength to have this same attitude toward your precious children. Accepting them without reservation for who they are without ignoring their improper attitudes and behavior will cause their self-esteem to soar.

2. *Self-Confidence.* Even before they walk, children begin to assert their desire to become independent. At around age two, this drive seems to blossom and is said to continue for several years. The "mother, please, I'd rather do it myself" stage often leaves exasperated mothers complaining about frustrating sessions with toddlers who fight to do everything themselves, from zipping a jacket when you're already late for a meeting to vacuuming the carpet with no regard for the toys or even the cat.

I have been able to cope more peacefully with this stage of development in our children as I have begun to see the need to build self-confidence. As I show respect for their desire to assert a healthy level of independence, they have learned to better understand their limitations. Children obviously need to have certain limits according to their age, especially when their health or safety is jeopardized, but in day-to-day activities it is important for them to try various things with supervision (such as tying a shoe, watering a plant, mowing the yard, or making the bed). One of several things will happen: they will realize that a task is too difficult and calmly allow an adult to take over; we will be surprised by their ability to succeed at something we assumed was impossible; or we will recognize our lack of training them to have responsibilities in the home (which begins in the toddler stage). In any case, we must be there to eagerly encourage them whether they succeed or fail. Encouragement is the key to building self-confidence because it will motivate them not to be moved by failure and, therefore, better prepare them for the more crucial tasks in later years.

3. *Respect for Others.* Galatians 6:7 says, "Whatever a man sows, this will he also reap." If we plant seeds of respect in our children, God promises that we will reap the harvest of respect from them.

Our nation is full of young people who have no respect for others, especially their parents. We assume that the problem lies in their selfishness and rebellion, and this is likely to be true in many cases. It is possible, however, that some of these young people have not had the example of parents who respected them as unique individuals. Therefore, they are unable to see the importance of this themselves. When a child grows up feeling like an insignificant nuisance, constantly being told to "shut up" and "go to your room," he will undoubtedly have difficulty having proper attitudes toward himself or others. Conversely, if he is given godly respect by those he desires so much to please, he will be better prepared to mirror this attitude for others.

4. *Loving Parent-Child Relationship.* When I was sixteen, my parents considered moving to another state. I was just about to enter high school and had lived in the same small town for twelve years. They approached me and asked how I felt about the move. I was blatantly opposed and begged them to let me live with my sister during the week to go to school and then drive over to be with them on weekends. Although they decided to go ahead with their plans despite my tearful protests, I was grateful that they had thought enough of me to ask for my input. Knowing that my ideas were important to my parents gave me the incentive to voice them when asked (and sometimes when not asked) and caused me to have a healthier

attitude toward their decisions. Children need to feel a part of the family. As we seek to show respect for their ideas and opinions, they will naturally begin to do the same for us and growing affection will be the pleasant result.

Seeing the importance of respecting our children is only the first step. Now we can explore some practical ways to tangibly express this important attitude toward them.

Verbal Affirmation

As we discussed in chapter six, being gracious and affirming with our speech will help assure our children that we love and respect them. Children are naturally very sensitive to the words they hear, especially from their parents. All too often we are quick to allow the first thing that comes to our mind proceed out of our mouth. Phrases like "please—you're getting on my nerves," or "if you ask one more question I'll explode," or "can't you see I'm busy?" would communicate a noncaring attitude to an adult as well as a child. Remember, "Pleasant words are a honeycomb, sweet to the soul and healing to the bones" (Prv 16:24).

Aggressive Listening

Have you ever tried to share an important idea or thought with someone who was obviously not listening? When this happens to me, I have a tendency to react two ways. First, I feel unimportant and discouraged. Second, I hesitate to go to that person again for fear of more rejection. To say we respect our children without being aggressive listeners is hypocritical. They must sense by our attitude as well as our "body language" that we are concerned about what they are saying, no matter how trite or insignificant it seems. Steady eye contact, leaning forward, touching their hand or shoulder, setting aside the newspaper, turning off the television, and giving them our undivided attention says, "I *really* care about you." In the hectic life of a busy mother, there will undoubtedly be times when this is impossible, but if we consciously make the effort, our children will come to appreciate us more and understand when they sometimes have to wait for a better time.

Positive Reinforcement

Positive reinforcement does wonders for one's self-worth. So often I am quick to detect negative behavior or attitudes in my children and quickly reprimand them for it. This is indeed one of my responsibilities as their mother, but certainly not at the expense of being just as eager to point out their positive qualities or ideas. It's amazing how enthusiastic Jaime gets when her behavior or idea gets a response of, "Punkin, that's wonderful! You're such a smart girl!" Acknowledging their affirmative qualities helps instill motivation in them to duplicate that behavior for more encouragement. What better way to let them know how very special they are!

Kept Promises

Have you ever noticed what a tremendous memory your child has when it comes to commitments you've made to him? They seem to easily forget to clean their room but are quick to remember that promise to go out for ice cream after dinner.

Keeping promises is another way to show respect for our children. Often I go to great inconvenience to fulfill a commitment to a friend, yet I expect the children to graciously understand when I'm too tired to make playdough or too busy to play house as I promised.

Benny has been such an example to me in this area. One Friday Joshua asked if he would go outside and help him ride his bike. We had recently taken the training wheels off, but he hadn't mastered it well enough to ride unsupervised. Benny explained that he couldn't do it that day but he would the following Monday, his day off. On Monday he was still recuperating from a weekend softball tournament where he had played for eight hours in temperatures of nearly 100 degrees. He was sunburned, exhausted, and feeling pain in muscles he never knew he had. Joshua, however, was raring to go. I was expecting Benny to explain that he would have to postpone helping him with his bike, but knowing it would be several days before his schedule would permit it, he kept his promise. Seeing him run down the street beside Joshua, knowing that he was sore and tired, warmed my heart. Developing this type of commitment when the children are young will prepare us for more important things in later years.

Before we glibly make promises to our children, we would do well to ask ourselves this question: Do I fully intend to carry out this commitment no matter what personal sacrifice or inconvenience it may cause? The security that they will have and the example we set will well be worth the effort.

"In the light of a [parent's] face is light, and his favor is like . . . the spring rain" (Prv 16:15). Respect for our children is important, but we must maintain balance, even in this area. In our zeal to treat them in a dignified manner, we must resist the tendency to go to an extreme. Allowing them to always "get their way" or catering to their every suggestion is not respecting them.

Isaiah 3:12 warns us that in the last days children will rule over or "oppress" those in authority. This is a dangerous trend. We must take seriously our biblical mandate to give our children the correction and direction they need without suppressing their need to feel like a vital part of the family.

Jesus, give me the wisdom and discernment to give my children the respect they deserve without minimizing my position as their mother. I desire to treat them with the same dignity that you did, knowing that you understand their needs even better than I do. I trust you to bring me to a place of balance in this area, Lord. Amen.

TEN

The Dangers of Comparisons

How I THANK THE LORD for my Mom and Dad! In his bountiful wisdom, God knew that with the personality and temperament he gave me, he would have to match me with parents who would motivate me always to do my best at whatever I set my mind. Their gentle proddings and encouragement forced me to recognize that God expected me to use the gifts he had given me to their fullest. At an early age I began to develop an intense desire to please my parents because I realized how much joy they received from my accomplishments.

I soon became somewhat of a perfectionist concerning my studies and felt that to be a good student I should get all As and Bs. This drive came from having an older brother who seemed to get excellent grades with little effort. I still remember the day I brought home my first C on a report card. I assumed that Mom and Dad would be very disappointed, put me on restrictions for the rest of my life, and confine me to my room with dozens of trigonometry books. Instead, they calmly inquired about the class, the teacher, and whether I felt I had deserved the grade I received. Naturally, I explained that the teacher was exasperating, the class was held during the sixth period when my brain was exhausted and . . . well . . . yes, I deserved the grade. By this time I was in tears as I told them of the times I neglected to study for a quiz because "Star Trek" was on or Benny and I just had to talk on the phone. Because I had set such high standards for myself, I felt that my parents would be as disappointed with me as I was.

In the midst of my inner struggle, Dad blessed me with an unexpected response to my report card. He said that they understood that math just was not my best subject, encouraged me to study harder, and praised me for my other grades. Their understanding was not based on accepting less than my best, but on realizing that in this case I had already dealt with the reasons why I had neglected to do my best.

As the years have since gone by, this and other childhood experiences have given me the assurance that my parents recognized me as an individual and did not necessarily expect me to perform well in all the same areas as my older siblings. Knowing that their love was not based on my following in my brother's footsteps concerning my scholastic accomplishments brought much security.

The key is to refrain from consciously comparing our children with others. It is an important, but often neglected, attitude mothers need to embrace. This does not mean we should accept each of our children's improper attitudes, lack of initiative, or negative behavior simply because "that's just the way they are." As we will see in the next section, all of these require prompt and consistent attention. Nor does it mean that we cannot be inwardly blessed by the admirable qualities we see in other children and deem them worth encouraging in our own. What this does mean, though, is that we recognize that our children are special individuals created by God with unique gifts, interests, and capabilities that will likely be different than those of his or her siblings and friends.

This tendency to compare our children with others begins at infancy. Subconsciously we use averages and norms to measure the development of our own children. Getting a first tooth, walking, saying a sentence, and potty training are some of the areas in which new mothers compare their little ones to others. The mother of a nine-month-old once asked me if she should be concerned because her baby had not shown any interest in walking.

Our Joshua did everything slightly before the averages recorded in all the baby books. He began teething at three months, walking at ten months, was verbalizing in clear, complete sentences at eighteen months and was potty trained at twenty-two months. Jaime developed somewhat differently. Her first tooth appeared at nine months, she walked at twelve months and at two and a half she finally left her diapers behind. Even when she was three, we still had to occasionally call on Joshua to interpret some of what she said.

From the beginning I have to admit that I subconsciously expected her to develop at the same rate her brother did in these and other areas and was somewhat concerned when she didn't, especially when friends began commenting on how hard she was to understand compared to Joshua. However, I soon realized that she was developing more quickly in areas like socializing, being more friendly and outgoing being more interested in helping Mommy around the house, and responding more positively to correction. Suddenly I saw that by expecting her to develop at the same rate in the same areas as Joshua did, I was unintentionally minimizing her ability to excel in other areas. What a joy it was to observe and encourage her exceptional qualities and stop being concerned that she wasn't talking as clearly as her brother or that she was still in diapers!

Comparing our children to others can cause several harmful reactions in them:

1. *Insecurity.* Whenever comparison occurs, someone comes out on the short end. Do you ever remember your parents or relatives making comments like, "Oh, but your sister *loved* playing the piano," or "Don't you want to go to college like your older brother did?" or "Honestly, why can't you sit quietly like Mrs. Smith's children?" Although well-meaning

parents may make these types of comments out of frustration or as a way to motivate a child lacking in initiative, what the child often feels is that he or she must meet the performance standards of others to be loved and accepted or that his or her parents would have been happier with someone else's children. The insecurity that will naturally follow can be devastating.

2. *Inability to discover their personal gifts, talents, and interests.* We are truly creatures of habit, even in the area of motherhood. It is so natural to steer our children in the same interests we had (or wish we had) and then to do the same for each subsequent child as well. My father was an excellent musician. He played the trumpet in jazz bands as a young man and had a beautiful baritone voice. Music was always a part of our home, and I appreciate the spectrum of music he exposed me to as a child. Piano lessons were offered to each of us as a part of his desire to father a musician. My brothers decided that sports were more fun, and my sister developed an interest in cosmetology. Finally, to Dad's delight, I came along and stuck with the piano until interest in school and boys began to develop, although my interest in music has continued to be a major part of my life. Offering a variety of interests for children to explore without allowing them to jump irresponsibly from one to the next as they get bored will provide the necessary opportunities for growth. Then, encouraging them in those they seem especially gifted insures that they will excel in their God-given talents. Expecting them to do well in certain areas simply because someone else in the family did can be both unfair and selfish. Try not to become too concerned if your aspiring young ballerina suddenly appears to be a gifted point guard on the girl's basketball team. Encourage her to be committed, to do her best, to take it seriously, and then scream your loudest for her at all the games. The discipline and character she receives are the most important things that come either way. *The Mother's Almanac,* by Marguerita Kelley and Elia Parsons, gives some excellent advice in this area:

The more your child is allowed to expand . . . the better he can express himself. While one child might speak best with words, another uses his easel or his carpenter's kit, and still another prefers clay or needle and thread or a suitcase full of dress-ups . . . his preferences often point out his talents. Unless he has the chance to sample a little bit of everything, he may never find out where these talents lie.

3. *Low self-esteem.* Children who feel that they are constantly disappointing their parents because they are not doing well in the areas they feel are important are often left with low self-esteem because they sense they have nothing within *themselves* to offer. As mothers we must be constantly seeking creative ways to *build up* our children by assuring them of our unconditional love. By encouraging their individual gifts, we will not only add diversity to the interests of our families, but we will also be allowing each child to shine in his or her special way. Four musicians in my family would have meant a lot of recitals and none of Randy's baseball games, Bonnie's hair-cutting experiments, and Jon's tinkering with car engines. The support and encouragement we received made us each feel that we could make a contribution to the family, thus building our self-esteem and feelings of importance.

4. *Envy and sibling rivalry.* Insecurity, lack of acknowledgement of individual gifts, and low self-image will ultimately lead to competition and jealousy in the family. In the nearly ten years we have been able to minister to teenagers, Benny and I have seen sibling rivalry as a very common problem, usually in the second, third, or succeeding children. A frustrated teenager once confided that he would never have his father's acceptance because he was not pursuing a medical career like his older brother. Obviously, this came from the perspective of a confused and sometimes irresponsible teenager, but he had undoubtedly perceived this attitude from his father in some way or another. The envy he felt toward his unsuspecting

brother caused a wall between them, and his athletic abilities were left unnoticed by his parents.

Proverbs 27:4 says, "Wrath is fierce and anger is a flood, but who can stand before jealousy?" When we sense that one of our children is envious of another, we would do well to make sure that we have pure hearts before the Lord in that we have not instigated this evidence of insecurity in the child by comparing him with others. One practical way we can ensure that each of our children knows we love and take pride in them is to be sensitive to the onlooking child when another is getting special attention.

When Joshua had just turned five, he made his decision to become a Christian and make Jesus "boss" (Lord) of his life. Needless to say, we were thrilled. Because of the excitement generated in our family and throughout our fellowship over his conversion, we wondered if Jaime felt somewhat left out, especially when she began to become unusually overt in her behavior to get our attention. Then when we purchased a Bible to give Joshua on the day he was baptized and planned a special lunch for our family members to honor him, we were again concerned that she may unintentionally resent all the attention he had been getting. Although we had often bought something special or needed for one and not the other, encouraging the one to be happy for the other, we wanted to be sensitive to her needs as well. The idea that came worked wonderfully.

The day I was preparing for the luncheon I told her how much I needed her help and found ways for her to help straighten the house and prepare the food. Then Benny and I explained that we had a big "secret" and showed her Joshua's Bible. We told her that this was a special gift to honor him and asked if she would please present it to him. She was delighted! We thanked and praised her for all her help and told her how we couldn't have done it without her. Although we wanted to give Joshua the Bible on Sunday morning before the meeting, she was too excited to wait. She got a box to put it in and ran outside to get him. It was a beautiful experience for us to see her so unselfishly happy for her brother. We were grateful to God for giving us such creative ways to offset any insecurity she may have had otherwise.

5. *Resentful or proud mother.* If we compare our children in a negative way to others, one will obviously come out on the short end as I have already mentioned. If this attitude of comparison in our hearts continues, the eventual result is that we unintentionally resent the one child for his lack and our perspective in the home is damaged. If we, on the other hand, compare our children in a positive way ("I'm glad my children don't behave like *that*")and continue with this attitude, we will have to eventually deal with a spirit of pride. Soon we are exalting ourselves and our children, only to find that, "Pride goes before destruction and haughtiness before a fall" (Prv 16:18, Living Bible).

Have you been sensing insecurity, lack of initiative, or jealousy in your children? Have you been feeling resentful at their lack of development in certain areas? Take a moment to stop and consider whether or not you have had a tendency to compare them to others. God has given (or will give) you the unique children he desires for you, equipped with the gifts and interests he desires for *you* to help cultivate in them.

Proverbs 22:6 exhorts us to, "Train up a child in the way he should go." So often we attempt to train our children in the way we went or we lump our children together and assume they are all to go in a certain direction, but God promises to bless us if we train each as individuals in the path chosen specifically for them.

> *God, I admit that I have sometimes had the tendency to compare my children with others. I need your wisdom to allow them to develop as individuals. Help me to be able to not only motivate them to excel, but also to be there to lovingly support them when they don't. Forgive me and help me to see them each as the precious gifts that they are. Thank you. Amen.*

ELEVEN

Children Take Time

IN THIS SECTION we will be considering some very important aspects of being a mother, including discipline, teaching, and providing a proper environment to encourage our children's commitment to Jesus Christ as Lord. Before we get into the specifics of these awesome responsibilities, it is important that we realize that anything valuable is also costly. The thing that is most valuable to parents is our time, and children take time.

Our "instant" society has forced us into an unconscious mindset of expecting everything to happen overnight. Everything from credit to oatmeal is available instantly. Americans, as a rule, live in a "grab all the gusto you can get" existence of rushing from one activity to the next, becoming very impatient when things don't happen fast enough. We instinctively operate in such a hurried fashion that our hand is on the horn before we know it as the car in front of us hesitates when the light turns green!

If we are not careful, we will begin to absorb this mentality concerning our children. There is no method of training children that works immediately. We have to be careful not to pick up and put down method after method when one doesn't produce results after a few attempts. Likewise we must resist the temptation to abandon God-given mandates simply because we cannot see immediate results. Obedient, responsive, disciplined children do not happen overnight, especially if there are years of incorrect training to counteract.

Recently an older mother approached me after a woman's meeting where I had spoken on the subject of motherhood. She was especially interested in the section on discipline.

"I really appreciate your ideas on this subject," she began, "but I've tried those things before and they just don't work."

I inquired about her children and found that she has several, the oldest a teenager and the youngest a toddler.

"Tell me, what specifically did you try to do and what happened?" I asked.

She had read a book on discipline and had asked the Lord to show her what he would have her implement in her home. She then began to work these changes into the home and, after a few weeks, saw no changes taking place in her children. They were still responding in the same negative ways as before and, in some cases, worse. In frustration she dismissed the ideas and gave up.

This is a very typical response to lack of immediate results. Our expectations soar when we see hope in a new method of training our children, but the hope vanishes when results don't come quickly.

Part of the reason for this is that many of us were ignorant of the costs of being a mother. Granted, some women become mothers unexpectedly, but many others plan on each child. Because we may have had little experience with young children and were unaware of the tremendous responsibility, the daily frustrations, and the amount of repetition the young mind needs, we are unprepared for the commitment involved in training them. Rather than recognize our own incapabilities and unwillingness to patiently "stick it out," we throw up our hands and quit. After all, "they didn't know my kid when they wrote this book."

Children *are* demanding! Being a mother is a twenty-four-hour-a-day responsibility. When the doctor handed Joshua to me for the first time, I had no idea what was in store for me.

But this I now know: the word of God is true. Our God is faithful. He never calls us to anything that he cannot enable us to carry out. From what I sow in my children I will reap a harvest. I am the best mother in the world for them by his grace.

The time that we invest in our children will accumulate dividends forever. They are truly an "assignment" from God and we are exhorted to "run with endurance the race that is set before us" (Heb 12:1).

As mothers we must curb our renegade tendency to substitute other things to pacify children's need for attention. Whether it's a cookie or the car keys, we often use "things" to occupy them when what they need is *us*.

Several months ago I was talking on the phone while trying to fix dinner. Benny was expected home soon and we had an evening meeting. The children had been down in the family room playing quietly. I turned to see Joshua standing by the kitchen counter.

"Mommy, excuse me," he said.

"Just a minute," I said to the person on the phone, "what do you want, Joshua?" My voice held a tinge of impatience at the interruption.

"I just want to love you, that's all," he responded.

Needless to say, I ended the conversation, convicted by my impatience, and embraced my son. I had assumed that he wanted to know where Daddy was or when dinner would be ready. Suddenly I realized that throughout the busy day I had taken no time to just "love" him. They had spent much of the afternoon playing and I had busied myself with countless household chores. Dinner was a little late that night, but we had a great time downstairs for a few precious minutes playing "mommies and daddies" (I was the baby).

Without belaboring the point, the issue of television is important here. The average child spends up to five and one half hours a day watching it. I admit, it's convenient to let Porky the Pig entertain the children while I prepare breakfast. But when children are being influenced so consistently by the media, they will inevitably absorb the message it presents. No wonder young people are so numb to certain moral issues, since many of them witness robberies, murders, sexual encounters, and violent behavior happening daily in their own homes! A brother once exhorted a group of Christians to only allow the family to watch activity on television that they would also allow to happen in their own living room. The hours our children spend watching television would be better spent by providing them with conversation, crafts, books, a visit to the park, household chores, or other creative and wholesome activities. The television can simply be another one of those "things" we offer to our children to entertain them when they need some time from us.

It is also important to invest time in each child *individually*, not just collectively. When Benny and I taught a class in our fellowship on teaching and training children, we asked the parents the question, "Do you feel that you spend adequate time alone with *each* of your children?" A majority of the parents, especially fathers, said no.

A reputable survey reported several years ago that the average American father spends only 37 seconds a day alone with his children. Mothers at home can see why this is true of fathers because of their need to provide for the family, thus spending up to ten hours a day away from them. But more and more mothers are also working outside the home, either by necessity or choice, so that this statistic may likely apply to a growing number of mothers as well. Those of us who work in the home are not totally exempt, however. Just because we do not have outside employment does not mean that we spend regular, undistracted time alone with each of our children. Being in the home with them on a daily basis can deceive us into assuming that we are actually spending *time* with them. Again, time is costly. Just the fact that we use the word "spend" in reference to time emphasizes its worth. How we take for granted the years we have with our children! Soon they are grown and we suddenly realize how much we missed. Many of us still have children who are young enough for us to appreciate now, before we are left to regret how much we took them for granted and remember how each one is a unique gift, holding a special place in our hearts.

This concept of spending time with the children individually is one we try to keep before us at our home. Often Benny will take Joshua to a breakfast meeting or Jaime to run an errand, or I will arrange for Joshua to go with me to the mall or Jaime will ride with me to deliver something to my mother's. Other times we will schedule special blocks of undistracted time with them at the lake, the firehouse, or the playground. We have fun singing in the car or talking about what they saw that day at the zoo. The important thing is that they feel special enough to be worth a little time with mom and dad.

When Joseph was an infant, I often had to resist feelings of entrapment and selfishness as my normally stimulating and socially active life was greatly altered. Getting out with four was certainly more difficult than with three! With additional children come additional sacrifices.

My emotions came to a head one afternoon when all I could find to eat for lunch was one piece of bread (a heel, no less!) and some peanut butter. There had been enough tuna for the older children, and nursing provided Joseph with the best for him whenever he wanted. But Mom was stuck with a half of a peanut butter sandwich. I began to remember the months of interrupted sleep, missed sermons, delayed showers, and cold dinners because the baby was hungry or needed changing. Self-pity was soon knocking at the door.

Selfishness is the most devastating threat against effective motherhood. Humanistic values would say the opposite, however. A popular attitude today is: "The most important person in your life is, and must be, you." What a contrast to the apostle Paul's exhortation in Philippians 2:3: "Do nothing from selfishness . . . but with humility of mind let each of you regard one another as more important than himself."

I was sharing this bout with my emotions in a home meeting

of our fellowship one night, asking for prayer for complete victory over selfishness in my life. Donna, an older woman with three grown children, one of whom was killed in an accident several years ago, gave me some excellent advice.

"Sheree," she said, "take it from a mother who has been there. All too quickly the baby will be grown and gone. You'll forget the sermons and the sleepless nights, but you'll never forget the moments you're sharing with him. Enjoy this time while you have it." There was that word again: *time*.

The last aspect of investing time in our children is maintaining the proper heart-attitudes as mothers. I once heard it said that children are like animals, they sense you like them. Although I laughed it off at the time, I have begun to realize the validity of this statement. If we spend time with our children with negative attitudes, they will sense this motivation. If we do so because we like them (that *philia*-love), they will also sense this.

Because mothers often spend the most time on a daily basis with the children, we tend to have a different outlook on our children than the relative who sees them twice a year, raves about how wonderfully behaved they are and how they would just *love* to have them come for the weekend sometime. The regular contact causes us to lose perspective and soon their flaws are so evident and their assets so hidden. This, in turn, affects our attitude and inevitably we become quite difficult to live with.

The book of Proverbs again addresses this issue using the same wording in two separate verses (21:9 and 25:24), where we read, "It is better to live in a corner of the roof, than in a house shared with a contentious woman." (I've often wondered if Solomon was motivated to record this verse twice by having some ornery wives.)

Webster defines the word contentious as "quarrelsome, belligerent, combative, faultfinding, militant." What a contrast to the qualities we are exhorted to pursue in 1 Peter 3:4:

"Be beautiful inside, in your hearts, with the lasting charm of a gentle and quiet spirit which is so precious to God" (Living Bible).

God is not asking you to become someone who never speaks above a whisper or who ignores the negative behavior in your children. He is concerned with your heart attitude. Do you *enjoy* the children he has given you? Do you take seriously your responsibility to train them to become responsible, godly young people?

As I mentioned earlier, the woman typically sets the "mood" in the home, while the husband sets the "pace." If I am irritable, impatient, or tense, the family seems to absorb my mood. If I am peaceful, patient, singing songs and laughing with my children, I am emotionally prepared for the events of the day and the family absorbs this mood as well. I am not saying it's my fault if Benny or the children are having a bad day or that the credit is mine if the day goes well. I am saying that the mood of the home largely depends on that of the mother or whoever spends the majority of the day there. Greeting Benny and the children with a smile or a frown will undoubtedly determine their response, which will in turn affect me and so on.

The time we spend cultivating our relationship with our children will greatly determine how they will develop in years to come. Patiently realizing that building character in them takes time, resisting the temptation to provide "things" to pacify them, committing ourselves to giving time to each child individually, and having loving attitudes when we are with them will help to make our times together more meaningful. The Lord once put it to me like this: "Sheree, would you like to have had the kind of mother you are?"

In the book, *Building Respect, Responsibility and Spiritual Values In Your Child*, Mike Phillips addresses this foundational point of spending time with our children. He speaks of the time we invest as:

Time that you will not have to give if you are busy with your own pursuits and ambitions. You must establish in your heart a commitment of time. Such a commitment can never be carried out from some lofty height of resolution. A promise of, "I'll do better this year," on New Year's Eve will not cure your ineffectiveness as a parent. Rather, it's a commitment you will have to make a dozen times a day.

I once read that "spending time means building memories." Memories are important to a child. As significant as it seemed at the time, I have forgotten the color of my room in junior high and the number of dresses in the closet. I've even lost sight of the disappointment of a girlfriend getting a new outfit or stereo when I didn't, as much of a crisis as it appeared to be back then. But I cherish vivid memories of vacations at Nags Head (where we now take our children each year), when Dad would hold me tightly because I was afraid of the ocean, of years of watching the fireworks at Greenbelt Park and the many nights when Mom would take the time to read me a bedtime Bible story. How this helps to give me a proper perspective on the value of providing such warm memories for my children!

Take just a moment to ask yourself these questions. How many times in the recent weeks have the children heard things like, "Not now, honey, I'm busy," or "Can't you see I'm trying to read?" or "I've had a long day; maybe later?"

How often are their naturally inquisitive minds met with "If you ask one more question I'll scream" or "What a silly question"?

How frequently is their need to be heard squelched with "I'm in the middle of something—can't this wait?"

Day after day, year after year they are hearing these things, but ultimately they are hearing "I don't have *time* for you." Then we are hurt and confused when suddenly, it seems, there's a distance between us.

Let's begin a new project today. Each time we're tempted to

conveniently brush our child aside, let's take stock of the situation. What's more important—the bathtub, the laundry, that phone call, or our child? The interruption will be worth the time. The time will be worth the investment. The investment will pay dividends forever.

Oh Lord, it's so good to be reminded that the greatest gift I can give my children is me! *Help me to have the right attitudes toward the time I spend with them and to be patient with the change I see as necessary in their lives. Give me creative ways to be an enjoyable mother so that I can build happy memories into their hearts of the few years we will have together. Amen.*

TWELVE

Do What I Say *and* What I Do

IT'S OVERWHELMING WHEN WE CONSIDER the amount of time we need to invest in our children, until we realize that much of that time covers the day-to-day happenings of life. Cleaning the toyroom, running errands, or giving them baths make up most of the time we spend with them. During these moments, we set examples that will permanently affect them. It is here that we must remember that our children will both intentionally and unintentionally learn to duplicate our behavior and attitudes.

When Joshua and Jaime were four and three, they started playing what would become a favorite game—"Benny and Sheree." One afternoon I sneaked downstairs to eavesdrop when "Benny" was taking "Sheree" out to dinner. He politely opened the car door and escorted her to their table (the fireplace hearth). They talked over dinner about various things, telephoned the sitter to check on the baby, and asked the waitress where the "potty" was. By this time I had moved from the stairway into viewing range of this humorous drama.

Just then "Benny" stood to reach for his wallet to pay for the check.

"Oh no!" he said, "I don't have any money. Sheree, do you?"

(He had undoubtedly remembered the evening we sat in the restaurant waiting for Dad to make an emergency run to the bank.)

"Sheree" then stood, thrust her hand on her hips and dramatically said, "Oh, Benny, you never leave me any money!"

By this time I was practically in tears with silent laughter, yet I had also received quite an education. Because adults are so much bigger in size, children tend to exaggerate their impressions of us. This incident, exaggerated as it was, nonetheless gave me insight into the example I was setting for my daughter.

Biblical Examples

Scripture gives us some additional insights into this concept of setting a proper example for our children.

In 1 Samuel 2-4, we read the account of Eli and Samuel and their sons. Eli was a godly man, a priest in the temple. He was given charge over Samuel by his mother, Hannah. Samuel grew to be a man of wisdom and faithfulness, yet "his sons . . . did not walk in his ways, but turned aside after dishonest gain and took bribes and perverted justice" (1 Sm 8:3). How could this be?

To discover the answer to this question we must look back into Eli's life, for he was Samuel's "father figure." Because Eli spent most of his time, love, and attention training Samuel as his "apprentice" in the temple, Samuel became a godly man. Yet the improper example Eli set as a father to his natural sons was duplicated by Samuel.

First Samuel 2:12 tells us that "the sons of Eli were worthless men; they did not know the Lord." Obviously, Eli was so busy serving God that he was not the father he should have been. His sons became involved in sexual immorality and began to use their position as his sons for personal gain. Eli, however, was so uninvolved in their personal lives that he was told *by others* what his sons were doing (v. 22). Many parents today find themselves in this same predicament. Preoccupied with their own lives, they are often shocked to discover "too late" what their children have become involved in.

In chapters 25-27 of Genesis, we learn another startling lesson of how our example can affect our children.

Isaac and Rebekah had twin sons, Jacob and Esau. Because Esau was born first, he was the rightful heir to his father's inheritance. Esau, however, forfeited his birthright to Jacob for a bowl of stew. Later, when Isaac was old and dying, Rebekah convinced Jacob, her favorite (25:28) to deceive his father into giving him the traditional blessing instead of Esau (27:8-17). The example of deception that Rebekah gave her son was a seed planted in his life. Genesis 31:20 records the heart-breaking result, "and Jacob deceived Laban," his father-in-law.

These two illustrations vividly portray the tragic effect that an improper parental example can have. Our children will ultimately duplicate the attitudes and behavior they see in the people they respect and love the most.

Attitudes and Behavior Are Learned by Example

Joshua has always deliberately tried to follow in his father's footsteps. Whether it's wearing the same cologne, going "jogging," or keeping his room neat, he has a tremendous desire to be like Benny. Unfortunately, a negative example can be as easily transmitted as a positive one.

When Joshua was three years old, Benny had taken him to run an errand. While they were crossing a busy intersection, a car started to cross into their lane. Benny blew his horn, but before he could say anything Joshua yelled, "Way to go, buddy!" Needless to say, Benny has made some changes in the way he responds to others while driving.

It is very important that parents realize that children *learn* attitudes and behavior. They are not born respectful, neat, and polite. We cannot expect positive qualities to be transmitted by osmosis, hoping that our children will somehow "turn out okay."

Our example will determine, to a great degree, how they develop. Whether it's the cleanliness of our homes or the way we respond to stress, our children will tend to duplicate what they see in us.

This principle of influence applies not only to the parent-child relationship, but also to the influence of the extended family. Just as physical characteristics seem to affect different family members, so different character qualities tend to be evident. Threads of alcoholism, sexual promiscuity, divorce, child abuse, or criminal behavior can be traced through the generations of some families, affecting great-granddad, then Uncle Buddy, later cousin George, then Mom, and finally, you. Similarly, qualities such as compassion for the handicapped, expressive physical affection, or strong moral values can be traced throughout other family trees. Less visible tendencies, both positive and negative, such as bitterness, tenderness, thoroughness, or jealousy, can also be seen by closer observation.

Why does this pattern arise? Because throughout the generations, children were exposed to the attitudes, values, and behavior of their family members. They began to see that certain things were acceptable even though they were improper. Recurring exposure to these influences helped to shape their attitudes, values, and behavior. Now we, by the same process, are influencing our children.

Several years ago Benny and I made a list of both positive and negative influences that each of our families offer our children. We prayed that God would provide a hedge of protection around them regarding the negatives and that he would equip us to capitalize on the positives. We were amazed at the things that came to mind as we began to examine the lives of our family members. If you do the same, remember that your desire is to learn from them, not become critical of them.

Children are quick to detect hypocrisy. How often did you hear "Do what I say, not what I do!" as a child? How often have you said it as a mother? How often have you had *reason* to say it?

Mothers are like fish in an aquarium. We are constantly being watched by little eyes. Soon we begin to see them mimic the example we have set. I often find myself doing things the way my own mother did, responding to the children or my husband the way she did and displaying attitudes I obviously saw in her. As Jaime gets older, I am beginning to notice similar things in her.

It is of vital importance that we maintain a posture of self-examination so that future generations will reap the blessings, not the curse, of our influence. Before we can expect our children to do what we say, *we* must first be willing to accept that standard for *ourselves*. Only as our actions are exemplary will our words be effective.

Modeling Godliness

In our home we often refer to "making Jesus happy" to help one another have incentive to be cooperative, diligent, or whatever the appropriate quality that is needed. When Joshua was four, he decided that he wanted a "job." This meant that he would need a lunch box and a briefcase like Dad's and that he would be gone a lot during the day. I convinced him that I would miss him too much for that, but that I was sure Daddy could find some jobs for him around the house.

Aside from his normal responsibilities with his room, toys, and taking out the garbage, Benny gave him his first paid job—carrying the laundry up from the basement. His salary was a nickel and was he proud. He carried it in his pocket for days and showed it to everyone.

That Sunday when it was time for the offering, I reached for my wallet to give the children some money. Then I saw Joshua reaching into his pocket. When the basket passed, he dropped in his nickel.

"Josh," I asked, "was that your special nickel you worked so hard for?"

"Yes, Mommy."

"You didn't have to put it in the offering. I would have given you some money," I said.

"I know," he responded, "but I knew Jesus would be happy if I gave him my own nickel."

"I'm sure he is!" I said, wondering if he could possibly be happier or more proud of my son than I was at that moment. I was also grateful that the example that had been set for him regarding the joy of giving financially had made a positive impact on his young mind.

Being Careful of Influences

An important responsibility we have as mothers is to ensure that the people our children are regularly exposed to offer the kind of models we want for them. Naturally we can't follow them around daily, isolating them from every negative influence. We can, however, take time to get to know potential friends, teachers, coaches, music instructors, babysitters, and other influential people. First Corinthians 15:33 gives us a sober warning: "Be not deceived; bad company corrupts good morals."

Children are like computers; everyone they come in contact with helps to "program" them. What is fed into their minds and hearts will eventually yield a "print-out." Protecting them from negative examples takes time and effort. It means interviewing teachers and requesting any necessary transfers. It may mean withdrawing your son from the soccer program or changing piano teachers. It also requires getting to know the neighborhood children and their parents, possibly directing your child away from improper relationships when necessary. It means studying the television guide to determine what programs are acceptable, and then not watching the unacceptable ones yourself! It means developing convictions about dating when the teenage years come and sticking to them no matter what. But your children are worth the effort. Sometimes I feel overwhelmed at the awesome responsibility of providing a proper example for my children. It's good to know that the God who gave them to me is also there to help me make the necessary changes in my life. How I long to say with Paul, "The things you have learned and received and heard and seen in me, practice these things; and the God of peace shall be with you" (Phil 4:9).

Jesus, I admit that I sometimes place expectations on my children that even I don't live up to. Help me to be the kind of example that they need. Protect them from negative influences and give me the strength to guide them by my life so my words will mean something. Thank you for your help. Amen.

THIRTEEN

Teaching: Assuming the Responsibility

PARENTING IN OUR COUNTRY has evolved to a place where many of us abdicate most, if not all, of our responsibility of teaching and training our children to others. Daycare centers or babysitters watch them when they are young; public schools teach them and the television entertains them. Many of us take little active interest in what they are learning and we feel we are adequately involved when we sign the report card or ask an occasional "How are you doing in history?"

This philosophy of minimal involvement contradicts not only the scriptures, but also American history as recent as this century. The center of education was always the home, even when public schools emerged, and parents (more specifically mothers) were responsible for overseeing the children's "lessons." The fathers discipled their sons into a trade, often their own, and the mothers taught their daughters about the responsibilities of homemaking and raising children. Formal education was confined to a limited number of hours for a limited number of years.

What a contrast to our contemporary society where many young people attend schools for twelve to sixteen years, logging some 18,000 hours in the classroom! We are a very educated people, yet crime, abortion, child abuse, divorce, and alcoholism continue to rise at astronomical rates.

My point is not that we should forsake our educational advancements and return to one-room schools. I am rather suggesting that although we have much "knowledge," we are not necessarily equipped to deal with everyday life. You may have progressed to the top in your field, make lots of money, and have a bright and promising future, but if your home is a wreck, you are undoubtedly a miserable person. Derek Prince, an internationally known Bible teacher from Cambridge University, once said, "You may succeed in every other area of life, but if you fail as a father [or mother], then in godly eyes you are a failure at life."

Our educational system is failing to produce adults equipped to effectively deal with life, not because the system itself is so terrible, but rather because parents regard it as sufficient rather than supplemental. You see, God gives *parents* primary responsibility for teaching their children. And guess what, mothers? Most of it lies with us.

Your immediate response to this chapter so far is probably something like this: "Come on, now. Are you trying to tell me that I should be teaching my kids reading, writing, and arithmetic? You've got to be kidding!"

Relax. Although many experts agree that a loving mother is a better than average teacher of her own children, these scholastic areas are not the ones I am primarily addressing. The areas I am more directly referring to, however, lie in *training* our children to develop into God's young people. This includes varying amounts of what we call "teaching."

The Greek word translated "teach" means "to give instruction or to train." Webster defines it as "to train, to give lessons to, to instruct, to provide with knowledge and insight."

Why are mothers more actively responsible in this area? Dr. Benjamin Spock, a man whose philosophies I cannot totally endorse, gives us a clue:

> There is no doubt that the personality of a child is more pliable in his early years, and that ... he is constantly being molded by his parents, especially his mother, or by the substitute who spends the most time with him.

As we have already seen, the most effective way we teach and train our children is by our example. Just as love is the foundation for discipline, so being a proper example is the foundation for teaching.

> My son, observe the commandment of your father, and do not forsake the teaching of your mother, . . . for the commandment is a lamp and the teaching is a light.
> (Prv 6:20, 23)

From this passage we see that, although the basic commandments (laws) of the home are the responsibility of the father to establish, the mother is instructed to support them through her "teaching," i.e., specific instructions to support the laws.

Let's say that your teenage son asks if he can use the car Friday night to go to a basketball game. The father gives him permission with the condition that he clean the garage to pay for the gas and that he complete a research paper due Monday morning. Because the father works each day, the mother is then left to support his decision by seeing that the son carries out the father's conditions. She must not give the son gas money if he and a friend get home too late from the library to clean the garage. It is his clear responsibility to organize his time to complete the assigned tasks before he is handed the keys to the car.

Notice what Paul wrote to Timothy:

> For I am mindful of the sincere faith within you, which first dwelt in your grandmother Lois, and your mother Eunice, and I am sure that it is in you as well. (2 Tm 1:5)

> Continue in the things you have learned and become convinced of, knowing from whom you have learned them; and that from childhood you have known the sacred writings which are able to give you the wisdom that leads to salvation. (2 Tm 3:14-15)

We can see from these scriptures that much of Paul's confidence in Timothy came from knowing that he had been trained from childhood by a godly mother and grandmother. He had been taught and instructed in the things of God and thus became a wise man. The qualities he gleaned from their commitment to train him in the Lord, not only made him a man of the scriptures, but also built character into his life. He became one of the pillars of the first-century church.

Proverbs 14:1 warns us that "The wise woman builds her house, but the foolish tears it down with her own hands." What is your "house?" Obviously, the writer was not referring to a literal structure of bricks and mortar. The inference here is to a different kind of "house," one made of people and not materials. Seeing it in this light helps us to see that our "house" is actually ourselves (our attitudes, goals, character qualities) and those of our families. God says that we have the capability of building or destroying our lives and the lives of those in our family. We have already discussed some ways that we can actually tear down our children through criticism, verbal and physical abuse, and negative comparison with others. The best way we can build is to take seriously our God-given responsibility to teach and train them.

Let's review Webster's threefold definition of teaching and see how we can view it practically.

1. "To train"—The concept of training is best seen in athletics. The runner stretches, runs, exercises, and eats properly day after day, week after week until he has "trained" his body to endure the pain and stress of running. As mothers, we act as our children's "trainer," coaching them in areas that

will produce the discipline necessary to develop the character qualities needed to endure the stress of living a holy life. This would include practical as well as spiritual areas.

2. "To instruct"—Instruction denotes teaching in the area of practical learning or "to give lessons." Regularly spending time with our children, reading them books that will instruct them, or assigning helpful projects as they get old enough is one way to instruct our children. Many church fellowships have helpful materials available for chidren of all ages in this area.

3. "To provide with knowledge and insight"—A good example of this aspect of teaching is found in Proverbs 31:1-9 where we read of the sayings of King Lemuel, based on "the oracle which his mother taught him."

As you can see, teaching children is a lifetime commitment. It requires daily consideration, consistency, and clarity. To suggest that we have "taught" our children to be neat and orderly by requiring that they keep a clean room is inadequate. We need to explain what we mean. When my mother used to inspect my room as a teenager, I knew that her definition of "clean" was more than just being tidy. She had explained to me many times that for my room to be clean it must be dusted and vacuumed, the closet must be straight, the drawers neat, the bed made and nothing "hiding" under the bed. Because she committed herself to defining clearly what she expected, she seldom had to discipline me for an incomplete job— although I'll never forget the day I brought a friend home and found the cluttered contents of my drawer in the middle of the room.

Are you beginning to see why mothers are given more responsibility in the area of teaching the children? Although fathers are given clear biblical oversight in the home and are far from exempt in the area of teaching the children, the daily contact that we mothers have requires a continuous input into our children's lives. If we do not meet their need, they will ultimately turn to others to receive the instruction and direction they desire.

In her book *The Creative Homemaker*, Mary LaGrand Bauma says:

> If we neglect our parental role, our children will take their direction from their peers. Many young people have no sense of direction today because they have been left to find guidance from [others].

If we do not offer the training that our children inwardly crave, they will begin to seek it from others. Whether it is in practical, emotional, or spiritual areas, they will sense that we are disinterested and will begin to gravitate to those who will take the interest. Sadly, those who end up taking the interest often offer the wrong kind of guidance.

Marilee Horton further illustrates this important point when she says:

> Many children, having gone off the deep end into drugs, crime, or sex, say that no one would listen to them at home. They form relationships that strongly resemble families, however harmful they may be, because their peers treat them as important.

Another confirmation is made by Mike Phillips:

> [The] mental doors [of my children] may not always be open. If I don't enter in to teach and mold them in those early years when they are the most pliable, others will. Someone will teach [them]—their hungry minds will see to that. And if I do not "feed" them, they will seek "food" elsewhere.

You may be asking, "How can I begin to practically apply

this principle of teaching my children on a regular basis? What specifically can I do?"

Over the last few years, I have identified four basic areas in which I am responsible for teaching my children: that they love the Lord and his word, that they respect and appreciate authority, that they see themselves as uniquely precious to God and to us, and that they develop godly character qualities.

Love of God and His Word

My maternal grandmother was a dear woman who had a contagious love for the Lord. As a young girl I made a commitment to learn to love him the way she did. I was struck by the intimacy of her relationship with him and desired to know him as personally as she did.

As mothers, our deepest desire should be to see our children come to have a binding relationship with Jesus Christ. The way we can best ensure this is to provoke them the way my grandmother did me, by giving them an example of someone who is visibly devoted to God. Sending them to the best Christian school, taking them to the fellowship with the most exciting children's ministry, and faithfully reading them story after story in the Bible will not produce lasting results in them if they don't sense our deep love for God. David spoke of those who seek God "with all their heart" (Ps 119:2) whose soul is "crushed with longing" for God (Ps 119:20) and who see their God as a "strength and shield" (Ps 28:7).

Just loving God in a visible and intimate way is only the beginning of teaching our children to do the same. We must have an equally important commitment to actually teaching them by instruction.

Psalm 19:7-11 promises us that if our children learn to love God and his laws, they will be converted, wise, happy, discerning, and righteous, will fear the Lord, and will have lives full of great rewards. Read that list again. What an exciting promise! Is there anything really worthwhile that is not included there? But they are not going to willingly and naturally seek to learn God's law by their own effort. In fact, they will naturally desire to disobey and disregard God because, like us, they have been born with a nature bent to do wrong.

One of the ways we have tried to help our children to learn of God's laws is by having them memorize scripture. When Joshua went through a bout with fear of the dark at bedtime, we almost resorted to leaving the light on. Then we realized this would start a trend that would be difficult to break. One night Benny was out of town at a conference when Joshua called me.

"Mommy, I'm scared," he whined. "Can you please turn the light on?"

"No, honey," I responded. "Remember, Daddy said that when we are afraid we pray and ask Jesus to help us." Suddenly I recalled a verse from childhood and said, "And the Bible says that when we are afraid we should trust in Jesus (Ps 56:3-4). Why don't we say that together?" Slowly we repeated, "When I am afraid I will trust in Jesus" several times. Only once since then has he called during the night, partially because he knew he wasn't going to get his way by convincing us to leave the light on and also because he now had a reminder that Jesus was with him, even in the dark.

There are many other ways that you can tangibly teach your children about God, such as with stories, songs, prayers, and by using life situations to speak of the nature of their loving Creator. Speaking of his tremendous sense of humor in creating such funny-looking animals while walking at the zoo gives our children an inside view of God that is quite different than the picture most people grow up with. As we have begun to implement these things in our home, the fruit has been overwhelming. Hearing the children remind us to pray for a passing ambulance, watching them clap and sing enthusiastically at meetings, or hearing them talk about Jesus to the lady in back of us at the grocery store brings me more joy than all that money could buy!

Respect and Appreciation for Authority

Our society is characterized by resistance to authority and disrespect for the importance of the family unit. A 1982 court decision in Connecticut has even given parents and children the right to divorce one another. How God's heart must break at this tragic trend.

As mothers, we must be reminded that respect for authority in our chidren will come best by seeing it in us. Complaining about dad's decisions, criticizing the President for every move, justifying our negligence when ticketed by a policeman, and verbally attacking a teacher for picking on "poor little Suzie" is not going to add at all to their appreciation for authority. The Bible offers a way that we can scripturally appeal to those in authority in our lives when we feel they have abused their leadership (see Esther 4:8, 5:8, 8:5 and Ruth 1:6-18).

Romans 13:1 shows us that anyone in authority has been placed there by God. Passages including Romans 1:30, 2 Timothy 3:2, and Titus 3:3 list disobedience to authority among sins like murder, adultery, hatred, wickedness, and deceit. Allowing our children to have improper attitudes in this area is encouraging them to walk on dangerous ground.

One of the best ways to prevent this is by being a proper example in our reactions during potentially stressful situations. At these times our children are keenly sensitive, waiting for our reaction. When stopped for speeding, we can grumble and excuse ourselves because we didn't want to be late for the dentist appointment, or we can humbly say, "Children, mommy disobeyed the law by going too fast. Isn't God good to give us policemen as friends to help us and correct us when we're wrong?" Or when you and your husband disagree over allowing your teenage son to go somewhere with a friend, you have several choices. You can defensively tell him you did "all you could" to convince dad to no avail, or you can encourage him to be grateful to God for a father who loves him enough to stand by his decisions, however unpopular. How we respond when the heat is on will greatly affect our children's view of authority.

By teaching them to respond to us and all in authority with gratitude, loyalty, and submissiveness, we will be teaching them one of life's greatest lessons, for if they learn to do so they will "be wise the rest of [their] days" (Prv 19:20).

Their Uniqueness to Us and to God

We have already seen how important self-esteem is to children and that we should never consciously compare them to others. Their uniqueness is a precious concept that we must effectively communicate to them without going overboard by giving them a "look who *I* am" mentality.

Imagine this: God has created billions of people. No two human beings look alike, and, even in the case of identical twins, there is a slight difference. What can you do with two eyes, a nose, and a mouth, over and over and over? But God loves us each so much that he savors our place in his heart by making us so different that no one is like us.

Our children need to understand how much they are loved by their Creator and by us. Verbal affirmation, frequent affection, loving discipline, and other creative ways to express our appreciation for them are helpful ways to teach them this principle.

Godly Character Qualities

One day I suddenly came up with a real revelation—children are not born neat, polite, obedient, and truthful. No wonder I was struggling with the task of building these qualities into my children! As I began to research the biblical qualities necessary to teach them, my first reaction was to become completely overwhelmed.

"Lord," I pleaded, "You're asking too much! *I* don't even have a lot of these qualities. How do you expect me to teach them to the children?"

It was almost as if I heard him say, "I've finally got you right where I want you. Of course you can't do it! Only as you realize your inability will I be able to help you."

I decided that God was right. My shortcomings were ever before me. I decided to make a list of qualities for the children and me to work on together. I started by explaining that we would work on developing one quality a month. Even though they couldn't understand what I was saying at first, they are beginning to understand more and more. After the explanation, I copied a related scripture onto three-by-five cards and posted them as personal reminders around the house. Each day I would be visually reminded to work on our quality for the month. I informed Benny of our project so that he could help reinforce the quality too. Together we would consistently confront the negative and praise the positive in each other and in the children. As we have worked on specific areas (politeness, gratefulness, truthfulness, and so on), we have noticed real growth in the entire family. In fact, we often get reminders from the children when we say, "yeah", instead of "yes," forget to say, "please," or neglect to put our shoes away when we straighten our room.

Here is a list of the qualities we researched as being important to teach our children. You might want to post them somewhere in your home to check off on a monthly basis.

Character Qualities

(2 Peter 1:8)

Qualities	*Negatives to look for*
Attentive (Prv 16:20-21, 25:12)	Distracted, impolite
Obedient (Ti 3:1)	Rebellious, resistant

Qualities	Negatives to look for
Truthful (Prv 12:19, 4:24)	Lying, deceitful, scheming
Punctual, dependable (Prv 20:6)	Tardy, procrastinating, undependable
Neat, organized (1 Cor 14:33, 40)	Disorganized, untidy
Grateful (Prv 6:34)	Demanding, discontent, jealous
Loyal, trustworthy (Prv 20:6)	Disloyal, taking advantage
Patient (Prv 16:32, 17:27, 14:17)	Quick-tempered, demanding
Forgiving (Mk 11:25)	Brooding, pouting, bitter
Respectful (Rom 13:1-2)	Disrespectful, resistant, arrogant, impolite
Compassionate (Prv 31:8-9)	Selfish, ignoring others, insensitive
Humble (Prv 15:33, 13:1, 12:15)	Proud, bragging, arrogant
Energetic (Prv 18:9)	Lazy, apathetic, unresponsive
Fearing God (Prv 16:6, 10:27)	Unresponsive spiritually

Qualities	*Negatives to look for*
Polite (Prv 20:5)	Cocky, disrespectful, interrupting often
Generous (Prv 3:27-28, 11:25)	Stingy, miserly, selfish
Diligent, thorough (Prv 21:5)	Hasty, leaving tasks incomplete

Accepting our biblical mandate to teach our children is an awesome responsibility that must be undertaken with full knowledge that our example will be the best teacher. God promises us that he will both equip and sustain us if we are faithful to respond with enthusiasm and humility (Jas 4:6).

Jesus, I'm amazed at how awesome the responsibilities of being a mother are. I ask for your help to offer my children the training and instruction they consistently need. Somehow I feel both overwhelmed and excited because it's a challenge that I know you and I can conquer together. *Amen.*

FOURTEEN

Loving through Discipline

ONE SPRING WE HAD A FAMILY gathering where dozens of relatives came together for a picnic in my mother's backyard. There was lots of food, fun, and children. Mom has a grassy hill in the yard with patches of dirt, formed from the adventures of the children she used to babysit, as well as from our children. They love to slide down the dusty place on their bottoms and drive their toy cars through the trails.

On the day of the picnic we arrived somewhat late and some of the children were already sliding down the hill.

"Children," I said to Joshua and Jaime, "we have to leave from here to go to a meeting so you may not slide down the hill because you will get all dirty. Okay?"

"Okay, Mommy," they agreed.

We had a wonderful afternoon and returned late that evening from the meeting. Mom called soon after we got the children into bed to tell us about a conversation she had overheard. An adult at the picnic had apparently heard me telling the children not to play on the hill and approached Joshua about it. He encouraged him to go ahead and slide on the hill with the other boys because I could easily wash his clothes.

When Mom heard his suggestion, she started to respond, but before she could, Joshua answered, "Oh no, I may not disobey Mommy," and walked away.

Although I was angered at an adult suggesting to a four-year-old child that he blatantly disobey a direct rule of his parents, Benny reminded me that God used this incident to test our son's loyalty. We were moved to tears by his attitude and immediately went to his room to praise him for such a wonderful response!

Had I been told years ago that our son would be capable of such loyalty, I would have hopelessly disagreed. So many times I have thought these recent years, "Lord, what's happening? This discipline just isn't working! The harder I try, the worse it seems to get." Once again I was forced into the scriptures to discover for myself what God's word has to say about this important aspect of training children.

Many excellent books have been written on this subject by experienced, respected Christian authors. The one that I would most heartily recommend, especially for parents of young children, is *God, The Rod, and Your Child's Bod* by Larry Tomczak (published by Fleming Revell and available at your local Christian bookstore). His insight will change your life and give you priceless resources to deal with the issue of "loving correction" in the home. He and his wife, Doris, live what they teach and have been able to be a positive example in our lives and the lives of many others. A plaque in their home says, "It is better to build children than repair men." Such is the motivation behind godly discipline: not to tear down by lashing out at irritating behavior, but to build up by instilling in our children the character qualities necessary for them to become Christlike adults whose lives will bring glory to God.

Because of the importance of this subject in building character in the lives of our children, I have devoted two chapters to it. This chapter will focus on laying foundations and offering practical insight, and the next one will deal with the fruit we can expect from our labor.

Love Is the Foundation

Before discipline can be effective, there must be a strong parental bond of love and acceptance. The purpose for inserting this chapter towards the end is to lay proper biblical foundations before any discussion on discipline. So many times we are quick to decide that what our children need is to be "properly disciplined." In fact, you may be one of those desperate mothers who have turned to this chapter first hoping to find some quick help. If so, please go back and start at the beginning, because if you neglect to first build that love foundation, any discipline will be ineffective. When a child is punished out of frustration, impatience, or anger, the results can be disastrous.

Marilee Horton supports this important concept when she says:

> In learning how to love our children it is essential that we learn the proper attitude, method and timing of discipline. The proper attitude must be love. We must believe, and the child must also believe, that we are correcting him because in the long run it will be good for him.

Hebrews 12:6 says, "For those whom the Lord loves he disciplines, and he scourges every son whom he receives." As God disciplines us, we need to discipline our children from a heart of selfless love.

"But, I just can't help it. I get angry when they get on my nerves and before I realize it I'm yelling or jerking them up for a spanking. I make threats I don't intend to carry out just to get them quiet. I admit I need help, but no matter how hard I try, I can't seem to control it." Does this sound like you?

I, too, struggle with my lack of patience with my children, but I have learned that there is hope. It's difficult to hold back the anger and frustration, but it is not impossible. You see, the problem is not that "we can't help it." If you are a Christian, you are indwelt by the Spirit of God. In Galatians 5:22-23 we read, "But the fruit of the Spirit is love, joy, peace, patience, kindness, goodness, faithfulness, gentleness, self-control." You are an heir of this fruit in your life because you have committed your life to the Giver of all good gifts.

You may be thinking, "Well, I would agree that kindness is one of my strong points, but patience? Not really. Besides, you can't be saying that we should have all of those qualities!"

Notice that the word "fruit" is presented in the singular, not the plural. It is all one beautifully wrapped package, complete with nine ingredients. We have access to all of these qualities, and only when we choose not to exercise them do we operate in impatience, anger, lack of self-control, and so on. To deny that you are capable of walking in this fruit is to deny that "with God all things are possible" (Mt 19:26).

To further illustrate this important point, imagine yourself busily preparing breakfast for your husband and three children. Suddenly the oatmeal boils over just as your daughter appears from the bathroom with mascara all over her face. Your teenage son, who should have been dressed thirty minutes ago, rushes downstairs in his pajamas to inform you that he will probably be needing a ride to school because dad used all the hot water and he just has to take a shower before school. Your seven-year-old calls from upstairs complaining because he can't find his shoes again, and the dog presents himself in the kitchen with mud caked all over his body. Just as you begin to lose it, the telephone rings. You suddenly remember that a lady from the civic association was supposed to call to give you the address of the meeting that afternoon, so you pick up the phone and pleasantly say, "Hello?"

What happened to all of the tension and impatience you were about ready to release? No doubt, it's still there, but at that point you chose not to show it. You could have ignored the ring, except that you had asked her to call. Or you could have answered with "*Why* are you calling me so early? It's 7 A.M. and I'm already having a terrible day, so forget your silly meeting!" Obviously, your respect for the person and your tactful composure would never allow for such behavior. But the unmistakable point is this: we can control our responses in potentially stressful situations. Therefore, in disciplining our children, we can choose to operate in the fruit of the Spirit of the loving God who lives in us.

What Is Biblical Discipline?

Let's begin with what discipline is *not*. It is not the deliberate intent to stifle the emotional growth of our children by reacting to all behavior that doesn't meet our expectations. This type of selfish response leads to an average of two million children being physically abused each year, of whom six thousand die. Our local paper featured a story of a father who literally beat his fifteen-month-old son to death just minutes from our home. His reason? The child cried too much. Aside from physical abuse, there are countless other young people suffering the tragic consequences of emotional abuse by parents who verbally assault them.

Vines Dictionary defines the Old Testament Hebrew word for discipline as "to chastise, restrain, rebuke; to warn." Gordon McDonald defines it as "the deliberate stress we introduce into our children's lives to stretch their capabilities for performance"; Larry Tomczak calls it "the Biblical procedure for training children in righteousness so that they will become self-disciplined individuals.... Discipline is what you do *for* a child. Punishment is what you do *to* a child."

Thus, discipline is the loving direction we give our children for defined reasons, applied with proper attitudes on a foundation of unconditional love.

Cautions regarding Words

As we have seen, discipline and punishment are related but different. One form of discipline is rebuking with words.

When a child's behavior does not warrant a spanking with the rod or some other form of punishment, words can sometimes suffice. But we must be very careful. We should choose our words carefully, selecting nonincriminating phrases, maintaining a proper attitude, and being careful with our tone of voice. Proverbs offers some excellent insights in this area:

> There is one who speaks rashly like a thrust of the sword, but the tongue of the wise brings healing. (Prv 12:18)
>
> [She] who restrains [her] words has knowledge and [she] who has a cool spirit has understanding. (Prv 17:27)
>
> Death and life are in the power of the tongue. (Prv 18:21a)

In James 3:2 we read, "If anyone can control his tongue, it proves that he has perfect control over himself in every other way" (Living Bible).

We see from these verses that our tongues are able to give life or death, to heal or destroy. Phrases like, "If I see that again I'll slap your face," or "I wish you had never been born," or "Why don't you just leave me alone, can't you see I'm busy?" have no place in the Christian home.

So how do we avoid such abusive language? If we use it, we must humbly ask for God's forgiveness and then begin relying on his grace to sustain us. The moment we are tempted to speak in a negative way to our children, we are to choose instead to speak positively. When we fail, we should ask for the child's forgiveness and then return to the Lord in confession and renewed determination.

One morning I had to ask for forgiveness for speaking in a negative way to Jaime. I was busy cleaning the upstairs bathroom when I heard one of the children knock over the fan in the hallway. I picked it up and reminded them to be very careful and not touch it. Several minutes later I got off the phone after a discouraging conversation to return to the cleaning. As I passed the fan I, too, knocked it over.

"What happened, Mommy?" Jaime called.

"Never mind, just play with your toys," I sharply responded.

As soon as I said it, I knew I was wrong. My response should have been to acknowledge that I had knocked the fan over and that mommies need to be careful, too. Instead, I excused my behavior and went on to my chores. When I tucked Jaime in for her nap several hours later, I knew I had to ask for her forgiveness.

"Jaime," I began, "Mommy was impatient with you earlier when you asked me what happened upstairs. Will you forgive me?"

As usual, she responded so lovingly. "Its's okay, Mommy. I forgive you."

Remember, we can verbally correct our children without humiliating or exasperating them if we are creative. Benny and I have developed rebukes that include phrases like, "You may not" instead of "No!" and "That's unacceptable behavior" rather than "You're getting on my nerves!" Be sensitive and pleasant in your verbal discipline without losing the firmness and confidence that your children need to see in your authority.

Another caution regarding the way we speak to our children concerns the importance of giving clear directions. Disciplining them for things that have not been clearly defined will only cause frustration. Similarly, making suggestions like "Honey, wouldn't you like to pick up your toys for Mommy?" or "Isn't it time to do your homework?" and then disciplining them for not responding properly will cause equal frustrations. Children should only be given a choice when you specifically desire to give them one. ("Would you like to color or work with playdough?" or "Do you want to wear the blue pants or the green ones?")

Let's take a look at one of the above illustrations used first as a suggestion and then as a command to compare the outcome:

Mother: (pleasantly) "Honey, wouldn't you please like to pick up your toys for Mommy?"

Child: "No, I'm not finished yet."
Mother: (firmly) "But it's lunchtime and you need to clean up."
Child: "I just got these cars out. Can't I play five more minutes?"
Mother: (sternly) "No! Put the toys away."
Child: (whining) "Please Mommy, can't I . . ."
Mother: (angrily) "Stop arguing and obey, or you'll get a spanking."
[An angry and frustrated mother and child spend an uncomfortable lunch together.]
Mother: (pleasantly) "Honey, in five minutes it will be time to clean up your toys. Then we'll have lunch."
[Five minutes later.]
Mother: (happily) "Time's up! Please put all of your toys away and come for lunch."
Child (example one): "Okay, Mommy." (example two): "But I'm not finished yet."
Mother: "You may play more later. You may not argue with Mommy. Put your toys away immediately or be disciplined."
[In either case, with discipline in example two or without it in example one, the child responds, and mother and child have a pleasant lunch together.]

Clear verbal guidelines are a must for effective discipline and a peaceful parent-child relationship.

The Importance of Parental Unity

If you are married, it is vital that you and your husband be in agreement concerning the discipline of the children. If you are a single mother living with a relative or roommate, it is equally important that you explain your convictions and solicit the support of those you live with to provide needed support in the home. Lack of unity presents a confusing picture to the children, and soon they discover that daddy doesn't enforce the same rules as mommy or vice versa. Insecurity ultimately develops in the children because they don't understand what is expected from them. They tend to alienate themselves from the stricter parent and disrespect the lenient one. Because children learn best from consistent repetition, it is important that you, not only agree on rules of discipline, but be determined to carry them out *each time* the need arises.

We were at the home of some close friends of ours one evening having dinner. When it was time for their oldest child to go to bed, the father proceeded to take him upstairs. It seems that a recent response of his was to prefer whichever parent was not preparing him for bed, so he began to react, crying for his mother to take him to bed. The father explained that Daddy would take him to bed this time and that he must change his attitude immediately. The child continued to cry, intensifying his call for Mommy. Out of compassion for her son and partial embarassment that we had witnessed the incident, she offered to take the son to bed.

"No, thank you," the father replied. "I'll handle this." He took the boy upstairs, punished him, and brought him down to say goodnight. He began to cry again, and the mother offered once more to take him to bed. The father again resisted, saying that he would take care of it and proceeded to lovingly insist that the crying would stop or more discipline would come. The child stopped crying, said goodnight to each of us, and went to bed. When they had gone upstairs, the mother admitted to us that she was weak in this area and we all thanked the Lord for a father who took seriously his responsibility to train his son.

In this case, the couple was in total agreement on their convictions on biblical discipline, but in this stressful time the mother was unsure of how to handle the situation at hand. Had she insisted on taking the child to bed, rejecting the father's desire to deal with the incident, she would have encouraged eventual strife between them and a sense of confusion for the child.

It is important that we not presume that our husbands

concur with our attitudes about discipline in the home. I have talked with many women who quickly say that this is true, but then show concern when they notice the children acting very unacceptably after a few hours with dad. Many couples so struggle in this area that it causes strain in their marriage or an unwillingness on the husband's part to spend any extended time with the children. A friend of mine with a two-year-old girl recently remarked how much Daddy enjoyed the child during his daily moments with her but how differently he sometimes felt after several hours with her! Often this occurs either because of limited amount of time fathers are able to spend alone with their children, or because of a lack of knowledge concerning what discipline problems the mother typically addresses. Consequently, the level of consistency the child is accustomed to regarding improper behavior and attitudes is not maintained. Therefore, as his patience decreases his tone of voice increases.

If you sense that this is a problem in your home, lovingly discuss it with your husband. Ask him to read this chapter on discipline and any other material you feel would be helpful. Then agree on a course of action. Share your ideas with other parents that you respect and ask them to point out any area in which they sense you need to grow.

Again, don't assume that you are in agreement, because "through presumption comes nothing but strife" (Prv 13:10).

Response of the Children to Defined Guidelines

Children should respond to clearly defined guidelines in three ways: willingly (Phil 2:14), completely (Col 3:20), and immediately (Mt 4:20). Delayed obedience should be treated as disobedience. Expecting these responses will develop proper character qualities in them including thoroughness, cheerfulness, and responsiveness.

Months ago a mother of a toddler in our community approached me concerning some frustrations she and her husband were having in disciplining their son. In discussing the situation, I was able to share these three important responses with her and encouraged her to begin to consistently train her son in them. Months later we were at the birthday party of another child in the fellowship when her son did something unacceptable that required her attention. I was delighted to see him respond in all three ways and encouraged her in her training of him. She excitedly shared how their consistent, loving discipline totally changed the atmosphere of their home in just a few short months.

The Rod of Correction

You may be thinking, "Is spanking really necessary? Many experts say it's not. Can't I just reason with my child?" The question for the conscientious Christian parent isn't What does this or that "expert" say? or How do we personally feel? but rather, What does God say? And he says that words are not always adequate: "A [child] will not be instructed by words alone; for though he understands, there will be no response" (Prv 29:19).

The scriptures also give us clear instruction concerning the command of God to use the rod of correction:

> Foolishness is bound up in the heart of a child; the rod of discipline will remove it far from him. (Prv 22:15)
>
> Do not hold back discipline from the child, although you beat [spank] him with the rod, he will not die. You shall beat [spank] him with the rod, and deliver his soul from Sheol [Hell]. (Prv 23:13-14)
>
> He who spares his rod hates his son, but he who loves him disciplines him diligently. (Prv 13:24)

Read also Proverbs 10:13; 15:5, 10; 14:3; 29:15; 13:24. Remember all discipline comes from the foundation of love.

Use of the rod will be effective as punishment only when the love bond is present. Otherwise it will only cause further rebellion. The Bible insures us success when we obey God's commands with proper attitudes.

Reasons for the Rod

Each set of parents must determine what they feel necessitates usage of the rod of correction. Benny and I have come to use it in the following situations:

1. Willful disobedience: when we have *clearly* defined a particular rule and warned them of the consequence of breaking it, and they disobey.

2. Improper attitudes: again, when we have *clearly* identified certain attitudes (whining unnecessarily or pouting, for example) as being unacceptable behavior, and they ignore a warning to change the attitude.

3. Disrespect: being impolite, interrupting, talking back, lying, and so on, after being reminded that they are being disrespectful.

4. Hurting others: again, the importance of *clear* instructions is the key.

Both attitudes and behavior must be equally and consistently addressed. Punishing a child for improper behavior without dealing with his negative attitudes is like using the lawn mower to get rid of the dandelions in your yard. Outwardly it appears that they are gone, but the roots underneath will soon produce more weeds. Until you get out the spade and work hard to dig up the roots, they will not only keep coming back but will also multiply. Next spring the yard will have twice as many dandelions. It takes time to rid your yard of weeds and money to fertilize it to produce the proper kind of grass.

Many parents are quick to deal with improper or unattractive behavior. Few are willing to make the sacrifices necessary to deal with attitudes. After all, it's much easier and seemingly more important to discipline a child for stealing or biting another child than to discipline him for pouting or being selfish. Also, you certainly won't get as much feedback from well-meaning friends and relatives for addressing the former as you are guaranteed to get for the latter. But those attitudes will eventually manifest themselves outwardly if left alone. A child who is characterized by selfishness may become an adult who is obsessed by material wealth to the degree that he doesn't care whom he hurts or on whom he walks to get it.

You may be wondering how to detect negative attitudes in your children. Different children manifest their attitudes in different ways, but here are some things to look for: excessive crying not related to pain or sickness, whining and pouting, temper tantrums that may include holding their breath or flopping on the floor, sassy tone of voice, arguing, ungratefulness, selfishness, not sharing, and rudely interrupting.

Before you begin dealing with any attitudes that you have previously ignored, clearly explain this change to the child and expect a time of adjustment and increased expression of the negative attitudes. Only loving and consistent discipline will produce changed attitudes.

Application of the Rod

How, when, with what, and where the rod is applied is as important as why it is used. First, it should be done *privately*. After approximately the eighteenth month, children are easily humiliated by public punishment. Second, it should be done *immediately* after the offense. Children have relatively short memories. Often we have had to pull off to the side of the road, hunt for a restroom in a shopping mall, or excuse ourselves from dinner with friends to apply necessary punishment to the children. It places us in an inconvenient position but ensures that they understand that unacceptable behavior will be dealt with and not forgotten. Third, a relatively flexible object like a wooden spoon or a rubber spatula should be used to cause pain without unnecessary stinging. Fourth, God gave a special place that is heavily padded on which to use the rod: the backside. Children should never be slapped on the face or spanked on the limbs. God intended for children to be disciplined in only one place.

It is important that we realize that punishment is intended to produce *restoration*, not undue pain, humiliation, or embarrassment.

Beginning and Ending

Punishment with the rod should always have a distinct beginning and ending. The beginning should include finding a private place (restroom, empty bedroom, car) and explaining why the rod is necessary. After the spanking, the ending should include affirming your love, the child asking for forgiveness, and any necessary restoration on his part. Here is an example of a typical session with our daughter:

Jaime displays a negative attitude toward Joshua while playing (grabs a toy from him or screams at him, for example).
Joshua tells her to tell Daddy (tattle-telling is unacceptable).
Jaime: Daddy, I've had a bad attitude toward Josh.
Daddy: What happens when you display a negative attitude?
Jaime: I get disciplined. (Benny takes her up to our bedroom, our designated correction room.)
Daddy: Why am I giving you a spanking, honey?
Jaime: Because I had a bad attitude.
Daddy: Yes and that's unacceptable, right?
Jaime: Right.
Daddy: Bend over the bed.
Benny applies the rod and Jaime cries. Benny embraces her until she finishes crying.
Daddy: Punkin, Daddy loves you very much but you were disobedient by having a negative attitude and you had to get a spanking. Do you understand?

Jaime: Yes, Daddy.
Daddy: (If she forgets the next step) What else?
Jaime: Thank you for correcting me. (A tip we received from a friend which is helping the children to learn to *appreciate* correction.)
Daddy: You're welcome. Now let's pray and ask Jesus to forgive you.
Jaime prays. (It's important for children to know that disobeying parents is ultimately disobeying God.)
Daddy: Now, what will you do?
Jaime: Talk to Joshua (goes downstairs). Joshua, I'm sorry I had a bad attitude and [grabbed the toy from you, etc.]. Will you forgive me?
Joshua: Yes.
They embrace.

A defined beginning and ending assures the child that the incident has been dealt with and is over with no lingering guilt for them or resentment for the parents.

Consistency Is the Key

In all discipline, consistency is the key. We must give the same punishment for the same offense without compromise.

It took three weeks of consistently punishing Joshua, sometimes more than once a night, before he stopped getting up for no reason after bedtime. We were often tempted to give up, especially when his behavior continued incessantly. By God's grace we didn't, and now he gets up only to use the bathroom.

Spanking a child for something today and letting it go tomorrow is very confusing to the child. Ignoring improper attitudes or behavior out of convenience (you're on the phone, a friend is over, you're in the grocery store) produces frustration and insecurity. Remember, Proverbs 13:24 says, "[She] who loves her [son] disciplines him diligently."

In his book *The Christian Counselor's Manual*, Jay Adams suggests that parents develop a "code of conduct" where offenses and corresponding punishment are listed and displayed, which is especially helpful for older children. This idea ensures that the child knows exactly what will happen when he disobeys clear instructions, and it provokes the parents to be consistent in punishing the child exactly the same for like offenses.

A caution is important here. Any activity done repeatedly, whether it's tying your shoes or locking the car door, soon becomes mechanical. After months of disciplining with the rod it can become easy to go through the entire process numbly and mechanically because we know it's the "right thing to do." Discipline, like any response to biblical principles, must be done in *faith*. We must be led and energized by God in this area as we would in all others. Consistency is important, but we must not become like robots carrying out a function and lose our reliance on the Holy Spirit. Reaching for the rod "without thinking" and losing faith in God's promises and in compassion for our children are good indications that this has happened.

Alternative Punishment

Finding alternatives for behavior which doesn't necessitate the rod is important. The rod should be used in predetermined situations only. Some alternatives we use or have heard used are: impounding a toy left out, confining a toddler to the couch for five to fifteen minutes when he is overly active but his behavior does not warrant a spanking, restricting activities or privileges, or paying for a broken window. Naturally, the age of the child will determine the punishment. Sending a child to his room or denying a meal is inadvisable because they begin to associate their room as a place of punishment (thus many children hate to go to bed) and skipping meals deprives them of necessary nutrition. We should seek more creative alternatives to use.

Who Is Responsible for Enforcing the Discipline?

Because this has been a book written to mothers, I have purposely limited my discussion primarily to our role in the lives of our children. However, at this point, I must address the father's role, for I believe that if there is a father in the home, he is primarily responsible for overseeing the discipline of the children. Isaiah 3:4-7, 12 offers a startling glimpse at our society. Notice especially, phrases like, "the youth will storm against the elder... their oppressors are children, and women rule over them." This absence of male leadership typifies our generation. Many men have reneged on their God-given responsibilities as head of the home, resulting in oppressive children and domineering women. Certainly the mother is to share in the discipline and punishment of the children and is the one to enforce it when the father is not at home, but God gives ultimate responsibility to the father. I urge you to look up the following passages concerning this issue: Psalm 78:5-7; Genesis 18:19; 1 Samuel 3:13.

Lovingly communicate with your husband, letting him know how much you and the children need his leadership and then allow him to be the head of your home.

"I will be his father... when he commits iniquity, I will chasten him with the rod of men" (2 Sm 7:14).

All of the above ingredients will provide an environment which will cultivate properly disciplined children. Children who are loved but not disciplined become spoiled and those who are disciplined but not loved become discouraged. An article in a nationally distributed newspaper even calls "lack of discipline" one of the major causes of stress in children, and points to future problems in mental or physical health that may result.

In discipline, it is important to remember that our purpose is not to break their spirit but their *will*. Proverbs 18:14 warns us that "the spirit of a [child] can endure his sickness but a broken spirit who can bear?" Sickness is easier for a child to bear than a broken heart.

Is God speaking to you to begin disciplining your children according to his pattern? Know that the road will be long, often inconvenient, and lacking in immediate results, but he will bless your commitment as you step out in faith, putting your hand to the plow without looking back. Count the costs and then step out. The results will come: he promises!

Jesus, thank you for such clear guidance in your word concerning discipline. I admit that I am not always loving and patient in correcting the children. I need your help so desperately in this area. Give me the strength and wisdom to consistently give them the discipline they need. Thank you, Lord. Amen.

FIFTEEN

The Fruit of Your Labor

SOME TIME AGO, Joshua and Jaime came out of the children's ministry time on Sunday morning with cups filled with dirt. They excitedly told how they had planted little seeds that would soon grow. For days the first thing they did each morning was to go downstairs to check their "gardens." We would water them faithfully and set them on the kitchen table in the sunshine.

After a few days they became impatient.

"Mommy," they asked, "What's wrong? The seeds aren't growing."

"Be patient and if we keep giving them water and sunshine, they'll grow," I responded, hoping that I hadn't killed them with too *much* water.

One morning we came downstairs and saw life coming through the soil. The children were delighted.

"Oh Mommy, look! They're growing! They're growing!" It was fun to share in their joy, and soon they rushed upstairs to tell the news to Daddy.

When healthy seeds are planted in rich soil, watered regularly, and given the proper amount of sun, they grow. Only when care is improper or inconsistent do they whither and die.

So it is with disciplining children. If we plant seeds of loving correction in their lives and maintain a commitment to consistency and unselfishness, God promises us results. The fruit will come! No, it won't happen immediately, and you must resist the discouragement that comes at the outset when all seems hopeless. Our kitchen table now proudly displays two flourishing little plants that will soon be planted outside because we didn't throw them out after a few disappointing days.

Almost every day I have occasion to talk with or observe frustrated mothers who feel they have already lost the battle before it has even begun. Out of a sense of hopelessness they either lash out at the children in anger or ignore their behavior, hoping no one will notice it. Whether it is at the pool or the grocery store, I want to say, "Please don't give up! There is hope! You are the very best mother for your child, and you *can* help him to overcome his negative behavior."

The philosophies of this world have offered no hope as expert after expert has shared an idea that produced no lasting results. Crime, immorality, alcohol and drug abuse, and rebellion to authority continue to climb among young people at epidemic rates.

Are you feeling this sense of hopelessness? Maybe even reading the previous chapter left you with the feeling of "I can't apply those principles. I've tried everything and, to be quite honest, I'm afraid to believe it will work for me. If I just had hope for tangible results."

God will honor your willingness to obey his instructions, and he promises you success. To help you build your faith, let's examine seven of many results of *consistent*, biblical discipline in the home.

True Repentance

When children are old enough for the first stages of punishment, they are unable to adequately verbalize, much less understand, the concept of repentance. As the months and years go by, it is important that they be taught that insincere apologies and avoiding spanking by acting properly when mom and dad are around is not enough. Someday, we will not be there to oversee all of their behavior. Our goal should be to build godly character into their lives so that they will be able to stand alone, if necessary, against the pressures they will undoubtedly face as the world demands a compromise on what they have been taught.

Loving correction and verbal explanation given consistently will eventually teach them that their behavior is not just unacceptable to their parents, but ultimately to God. The discipline we provide should lead them to a place of repentance and changed behavior, thus ensuring that they will be loyal when we are not around.

Second Corinthians 7:9-10 in the Amplified Bible says:

> Yet I am glad now, not because you were pained, but because you were pained unto repentance... for godly grief ... produces a repentance that leads and contributes to salvation and deliverance from evil and it never brings regret.

Although the context of this passage does not refer to training children, we can glean from it that the discipline we provide, although momentarily painful for us and our children, will produce not just outward changes but changes of the heart leading to salvation. What a promise!

Changed Behavior

If you are the mother of younger children, hearing promises about heart changes in the future is great, but does little to help you deal with today. Know that the second product of biblical discipline can bring you hope, for changed behavior will come from consistent correction.

Children must be lovingly confronted by their improper behavior and attitudes time after time, day after day, before change will come. Soon the proper behavior and attitudes become "natural," and change is permanent. Not punishing a child because "that's just the way he is" or because we don't want to "damage his personality" is selfish. Ultimately, we must admit that too often we neglect to discipline the child, not out of concern for him, but because it's easier to ignore it. Consistent correction is much harder for us to give than for him to receive.

Roy Lesin speaks of parents who:

> choose to withhold the brief moment of pain needed for correction and allow children to continue on in attitudes and actions that will affect their well-being throughout life. To refuse to discipline children is a clear sign that we do not have the love God wants us to have for [them].

"Being punished isn't enjoyable when it is happening—it hurts! But afterwards we can see the result, a quiet growth in grace and character" (Heb 12:11, Living Bible). When it took three weeks to overcome the problem of Joshua getting out of bed needlessly, we were exhausted. But it produced results that have continued, and now it has become "natural" for him to remain in his bed.

Relief of Guilt and a Clear Conscience

I'll never forget the day I skipped school in my senior year of high school. Spring fever and the "senior slump" had captured everyone. One gorgeous morning, some of us began to talk at the water fountain about how much fun it would be to go to the park for the day. I had never skipped a day of school because my parents were very strict about such things and I had seen my brother punished many times for doing it. I was getting a lot of pressure to go, especially from my eventual husband, and it didn't take too long to convince me, especially since I was the only one who had driven to school.

Everyone had a great time that day, but I was uneasy. When I got home, I defensively reacted to Moms innocent inquiries about my day, suspecting that she somehow knew (my sunburn was a big clue). By bedtime, I was miserable and finally went in to my parents to confess what I had done. They lovingly rebuked me by reminding me of my commitment to not drive anywhere other than to school and back and calmly took my keys for a week. I was so relieved! I went to sleep and no longer fought feelings of guilt for blatantly rebelling against them.

I am still eager to learn how my parents were able to instill such loyalty in me, but the fact is: discipline relieves guilt. Inconsistent punishment *produces* guilt because the child is left to justify himself and wonder if he will be able to get away with the behavior the next time. After years of no discipline, he will develop a dull conscience.

In Acts 23:1, Paul claimed that he had "always lived before God with a clear conscience." Paul had hardly lived a perfect life. He had been responsible for murdering Christians before his conversion. How dare he boast of always having a clear conscience before God!

Paul had learned an important concept. When he turned to God in confession and repentance of his sins, he was cleansed and forgiven. He no longer bore the guilt of them. God says he forgives and forgets our sin.

When we do not lovingly punish our children, we leave them in their guilt, but when we discipline them, we leave them free to have a clear conscience. "He who conceals his transgressions will not prosper, but he who confesses and forsakes them will find compassion" (Prv 28:13).

Peace in the Home

If there is anything our homes need, it is peace. Many women resort to outside employment, not because the family cannot survive without the additional income, but because they are unable to cope with the daily chaos in the home. Ultimately, they conclude that they must not be cut out for full-time motherhood and surmise that the children would be better off in another setting with a more qualified person. A neighbor told me one summer that she couldn't wait until she could get back to work after the birth of her second child because her toddler was "driving her crazy."

Peace in the home can be greatly enhanced by commitment to faithful discipline. At first, chaos seems to increase as parents are trying new things and disciplining for previously ignored behavior and attitudes. The children react to the point that their behavior temporarily worsens. At that time, you will be tempted to give up. But press on! At the very moment you want to throw up your hands and quit, know that success is just around the corner. As you maintain loving correction despite the initial frustrations, God will honor and bless you because you have been obedient to his principles. Psalm 119:165 promises us that "Those who love thy laws have great peace, and nothing causes them to stumble."

Tension and upheaval in the home accelerates improper attitudes in both parents and children. Picture it as a cycle:

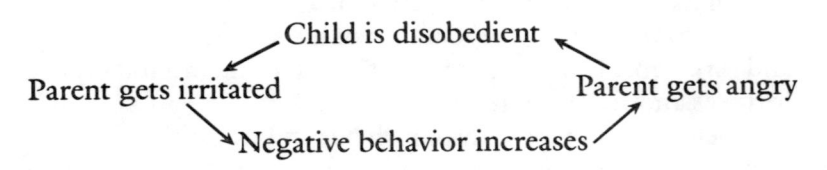

```
            Child is disobedient
           ↗                    ↘
Parent gets irritated            Parent gets angry
           ↖                    ↙
            Negative behavior increases
```

Studies done at University of Maryland and reported in Cliff Yudell's *Reader's Digest* article led researchers to an amazing conclusion concerning the "Battered Parent Syndrome." They identified the *primary* cause of this violence in children as "lack of authority." The researchers explained it this way:

> In the families we've seen ... there is one disturbance in the authority hierarchy. Usually one or both parents have

abdicated the executive position. The majority shy away from firmly stating that they, rather than their children, should set the rules. A substantial number even acknowledged that the adolescent is in charge of the family.

It starts early.... For many reasons, parents just don't assume their rightful authority in the home.... Youngsters need firm structure. They may object verbally, but that's what they want. And parents aren't providing it.

Let's look at the cycle when appropriate action by the parents, even if it takes more than once, is given. How different the diagram looks then:

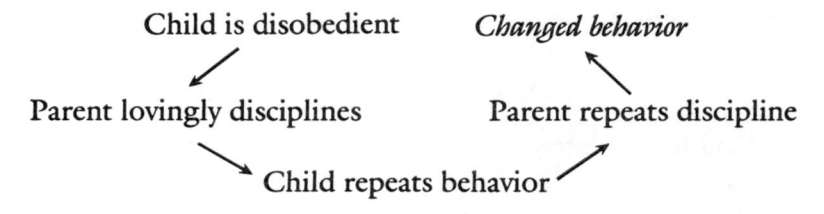

Child is disobedient → Parent lovingly disciplines → Child repeats behavior → Parent repeats discipline → *Changed behavior*

"The work of righteousness [which, for mothers, includes biblical discipline] will be peace ... quietness and confidence forever. Then my people will live in peaceful habitation and in secure dwellings and undisturbed resting places" (Is 32: 17-18).

Respect for Authority

First Peter 2:14 instructs us that God has placed those in authority "for the punishment of evildoers and the praise of those who do right." This give us an insight into why resistance to authority (government, parents, employers, law enforcers, spiritual leadership) is so rampant in our day. Those in authority have been inadequate in both punishing and encouraging those under their care. As mothers, we are no exception.

When our children go unpunished for things their consciences tell them are wrong, they soon become insecure and begin to disrespect our authority. They may unconsciously think, "I've done something wrong. Why isn't mom doing anything?" I have talked with countless people, including my own husband, who have admitted to acting improperly as youngsters just to get attention, even if it were punishment. Unfair or excessive discipline has the same effect, however. When a child is given unattainable expectations and then punished severely for not reaching them, disrespect for authority is also the result. Hebrews 12:9 refers to the respect that comes from parental discipline. Respect for authority in our children must begin in the home. From there it will become a lifestyle.

Secure, Obedient, and Happy Children

God has an interesting way to give Benny and me opportunities to evangelize. Recently, we were in a local restaurant with the children having dinner. Our waiter was pleasant, efficient, and seemed to enjoy talking with the children. When we were waiting to pay the check, he approached us and commented how happy and well-behaved the children were (they had been especially cooperative that evening).

"How do you do it?" he asked. Benny was able to begin sharing that we were Christians and that because we have made a commitment to God's principles for raising our children, he has made a real difference in our home. One at a time, the other employees began to gather around, customers started listening, and before long, the manager came to break up all the commotion. This was one of the many times that God used our children to open a door for us to share what he has done in our lives with others.

Consistent, loving discipline builds a sense of security in our children and, therefore, provides an environment where they are happy and peaceful. Not knowing what is expected causes them to be confused, and inconsistency fosters insecurity. We have been given the opportunity to build character into them through our encouragement and correction, thus insuring that they are well-adjusted and content.

From Psalm 32:8-9, we can absorb for our children God's promise for us, his children, which says:

> I will instruct you and teach you in the way you should go; I will counsel you with My eye upon you. Do not be as the horse or as the mule which have no understanding, whose trappings include bit and bridle to hold them in check.

In Proverbs 11:14, we are warned, "Where there is no guidance, the people [children] fall." As we accept our God-given mandate to instruct, teach, and counsel our children verbally and through faithful discipline, they will not have to turn to other things to "hold them in check" or fear "falling." Their happiness and contentment will be another promised result.

Growing Affection in the Home

When we first began to use the rod of correction with our children, their reaction was one of withdrawal and anger. Although we would embrace them and verbally affirm our love and acceptance, they would stiffen and try to back away. After a few spankings and our consistent affection afterwards, they began to respond both verbally and physically. Faithful and loving correction has given them tangible assurance of our unconditional acceptance, even when they act unbecomingly.

Remember, Proverbs 13:24 (Living Bible) says, "If you refuse to discipline your son, it proves you don't love him; for if you love him you will be prompt to punish him." Loving our children includes disciplining them when they fail to obey our standards of attitudes and conduct. As they sense that we are selflessly committed to doing what is *best for them* by laying down our time and energy faithfully to correct and encourage them, they will begin to have an overwhelming sense of our love.

Assurance that our children understand this important truth came pleasantly clear to me one day when I overheard Jaime "disciplining" one of her apparently "disobedient" dolls. As I walked into the room, she was saying, "Mommy has to discipline you because I love you and I want you to grow up to be happy, okay?" After she applied the "rod" (a pencil), she embraced the doll and again affirmed her love. I was so thrilled to have been able to view this exchange, because it gave me confidence that our discipline was perceived as an act of love for our daughter.

Below is a summary of the information in these two crucial chapters that you may want to copy and post somewhere in your home for daily reference (refrigerator, bathroom or bedroom mirror, etc.):

1. All discipline must be based on a foundation of unconditional love and acceptance (Heb 12:6).

2. Never punish out of anger, frustration, or embarrassment (Prv 16:32).

3. Respond, don't react!

4. Always be consistent, no matter how inconvenient (Prv 13:24).

5. Develop house rules or "code of conduct" with your husband and *clearly* explain it to the children (Am 3:3).

6. Have a beginning (clear explanation) and ending (restoration and affection).

7. Use a neutral object for spanking (Prv 22:15).

8. Maintain a "cool" spirit (Prv 17:27).

9. Expect them to respond willingly (Phil 2:14), completely (Col 3:20), and immediately (Mt 4:20).

10. Use the rod privately, immediately, and in the designated area.

11. Don't give up! The fruit will come with consistency and endurance (Gal 6:9).

12. Encourage positive behavior (Prv 16:15).
13. Discipline in faith, not mechanically.

Call to Commitment

God has clearly instructed us in how to discipline and train our children. Yet worldly philosophies and humanistic values seek to seduce us away from his ways. A simple, yet necessary, question to ask yourself is this: will I obey God? Your answer will determine the seriousness of your commitment to biblical discipline. Will you agree with the apostles when they said, "We must obey God rather than men" (Acts 5:29)?

God entrusts our children to us, instructs us in caring for them, equips us with his Spirit, and then promises us all of the grace needed to nurture them into productive adulthood. But so often we think, "But God, you don't understand! I appreciate you for giving my child to me, but I really think I should do things *my* way." Then, when the child becomes rebellious or gets involved in worldly activities, we turn back to God in anger.

When we realize, however, that our children belong to the One who created them and that we have been given *stewardship* over them, it's much easier to walk in obedience. The commitment we have to training them *God's* way will greatly determine their destiny.

As we come to an end in this consideration of discipline in the home, I challenge you to make a fresh commitment to obeying God in this area. Whether you already use the rod of correction in your home or have never used it, let's agree in prayer together that beginning right now, you will commit yourself to aggressively seek the Lord concerning this important responsibility. As we pray together, know that God will hear and answer.

And let us not lose heart in doing good, for in due time we shall reap if we do not grow weary. (Gal 6:9)

Lord, thank you for the assurance that consistent, loving discipline will produce fruit in my home. I now accept your mandate to discipline the children according to your guidelines for molding proper attitudes. Help me when I'm tempted not to fulfill this commitment. I really do want the best for my family. Amen.

Suggestions for Further Reading

Mary LaGrand Bauma. *The Creative Homemaker.* Minneapolis: Bethany Fellowship.

Elisabeth Elliot. *Let Me Be a Woman.* Wheaton, Ill.: Tyndale House.

Don Highlander. *Positive Parenting.* Waco: Word Books.

Marilee Horton. *Free to Stay at Home.* Waco: Word Books.

Beverly LaHaye. *I Am a Woman by God's Design.* Old Tappan, N.J.: Fleming H. Revell.

Beverly LaHaye. *The Spirit-Controlled Woman.* Irvine, Cal.: Harvest House.

Karen Burton Mains. *Open Heart, Open Home.* Elgin, Ill.: David C. Cook Publishing Co.

Jack and Carole Mayhall. *Marriage Takes More Than Love.* Colorado Springs: NavPress.

Gordon McDonald. *The Effective Father.* Wheaton, Ill.: Tyndale House.

Raymond and Dorothy Moore. *Home-Spun Schools.* Waco: Word Books.

Mike Phillips. *Building Respect, Responsibility and Spiritual Values in Your Child.* Minneapolis: Bethany Fellowship.

Larry Tomczak. *God, the Rod, and Your Child's Bod: The Art of Loving Correction for Christian Parents.* Old Tappan, N.J.: Fleming H. Revell.

Other Books of Interest

The Facts About Your Feelings
What Every Woman Should Know
By Therese Cirner

Practical help for solving the mystery of emotions. Offers encouragement and tested wisdom to help women understand, control and creatively channel their emotions. A lifelong resource for woman of every age and background. It is an excellent book for personal use and for use by small groups. $4.95

Do You Feel Alone in the Spirit
By Ruth Sanford

Loving God doesn't have to conflict with loving your husband. This best-selling book has helped thousands of women overcome the loneliness and discouragement that often comes when their husbands do not share their commitment to Christ. $4.95

Available at your Christian Bookstore or from:
Servant Publications, Dept. 209, P.O. Box 7455,
Ann Arbor, MI 48107
Please include payment plus $.75 per book
for postage and handling
*Send for your FREE catalog of Christian
books, music, and cassettes.*

MOTHERS AT THE HEART OF LIFE